Christ the Placenta

Christ the Placenta:

Letters to My Mentor on Religious Education

DAVID ARTHUR BICKIMER

Religious Education Press
Birmingham, Alabama

Copyright © 1983 by Religious Education Press
All rights reserved

Library of Congress Cataloging in Publication Data

Bickimer, David A.
   Christ the placenta.

   Includes bibliographical references.
   1. Christian education—Philosophy.   I. Title.
BV1464.B53   1983   207   82-24097
ISBN 0-89135-034-9

Religious Education Press, Inc.
1531 Wellington Road
Birmingham, Alabama 35209
10 9 8 7 6 5 4 3 2

Religious Education Press publishes books exclusively in religious education and in areas closely related to religious education. It is committed to enhancing and professionalizing religious education through the publication of serious, significant, and scholarly works.

PUBLISHER TO THE PROFESSION

TO MY PARENTS, ARTHUR AND MARTHA BICKIMER,
WHO BESTOWED A FAITH SO STRONG THAT EVEN THE MOST
RECALCITRANT OF NATURES COULD NOT RESIST.

Contents

Foreword

"But what can a book with such a title be *about?*" For those of you who have browsed this far in an attempt to find at least a beginning answer to that question, here are a few thoughts from one who has read what you may choose to read.

This is first and foremost a treatise about teaching and teachers. When the author says, "The most important career in the world is that of teacher," he plants his flag firmly in the soil of the reader's mind. For him, what a teacher holds out to a student is precisely what the Spirit holds out to man—"the promise of learning" with all of its probabilities of pain and delight and revelation. David Bickimer, *teacher*. He would want no other word placed beside his name to describe his human occupation. And while the book seems to be a series of letters from the author, as student, to his own mentor, it inevitably becomes a series of letters from the author, as teacher, to the reader, as students.

This is not a literary conceit, but rather a tribute to the eternal duality of man's quest as learner and teacher through the days and weeks and months and years of a life. The author dares to suggest that the teacher comes first, that we must ask how we can help teachers meet their needs even before we consider the needs of learners. This radical point of view coincides with that of Seymour Sarason in *The Culture of the School and the Problem of Change*. Sarason argues that as long as we say that schools are for students we will continue to ignore the needs of teachers to learn and grow, and we will continue to organize and operate schools that cheat children with tired, bored, and restless teachers. Certainly Sarason would agree with Bickimer's belief that those who would help teachers must identify and meet their own needs first. This admonition would seem to me to be as important in religious as in secular institutions.

The theme of *Christ the Placenta* is transcendence. Bickimer sees religion as the attempt of human beings to get in touch with something larger, to seek peak moments in life, to transform the rigors of daily life into mystical experiences. He does not separate this search into religious and secular pigeonholes; to the contrary, he urges the reader to find transcendental encounters as often behind the office desk as in the church pew. In doing so he stays in contact with what I assess to be a persistent if often thwarted need of every human being, in every station of life. We see this need clearly as people react to the art that comes before them.

I have always believed that the work of Thornton Wilder has sustained its appeal because the issue of transcendence lies at the heart of his best stories, novels, and plays. Nowhere is this more apparent than at the beginning of the third act of *Our Town* on a windy hilltop, full of mountain laurel and lilac, next to Mount Monadnock and high above Grover's Corners. The Stage Manager is walking among the cemetery stones:

> Now there are some things we all know but we don't take'm out and look at'm very often. We all know that something is *eternal*. And it ain't earth, and it ain't even the stars—everybody knows in their bones that something is eternal, and that *something* has to do with human being. All the greatest people ever lived have been telling us that for five thousand years and yet you'd be surprised how people are always letting go of that fact.

He explains that the dead lost interest in the earth and the family and friends they have known there, and something else demands their attention.

They're waitin.' They're waitin' for something they feel is comin.' Something important and great. Aren't they waitin' for the eternal part in them to come out—clear?

It is this "eternal part" in each of us that is of consuming interest to the author, and he wants us to discover how to let it "come out" in this world and not the next. Small wonder that while critics sneer at its simplicity, *Our Town* has become a revered play in the heartland of America that knows no geographic constraints.

I do not believe I am quibbling when I suggest that the subtitle of this volume (*Letters to My Mentor on Religious Education*) is somewhat misleading. This is a book with a number of important messages for all educators—whether they are parents or teachers or administrators, and whether they ply their daily work in religious or public schools. As a former teacher, principal, and superintendent in both public and non-public school settings, I sense that I have as much to learn (and as much a need to learn) from Bickimer about teaching and learning and the nature of education and transcendence as has a colleague who has always worked in religious schools. This book certainly is about religious education, but in a much more fundamental sense it is about education.

The commentary on Chester Barnard and Abraham Maslow is certain to be of interest to social scientists. David Bickimer wrote a definitive study of Barnard's *The Functions of the Executive* (which unfortunately remains unpublished in the stacks of Regenstein Library at the University of Chicago with a multitude of less important doctoral dissertations), and in these pages he reveals aspects of the thinking of the former president of New Jersey Bell Telephone Company which have been underestimated or misunderstood by organizational theorists. Here, too, we have careful attention paid to Maslow's *Eupsychian Management,* a remarkable and overlooked journal that psychologists have tended to reject as the ramblings rather than culminating insights of an aging scholar—peak experiences, if you will. We can only hope for a more detailed future exploration by Bickimer of the intersecting ideas of these two men of vision, both fearless in the face of the nonlogical.

You will wince several times in the early pages of this book. The author is convinced that deeply personal statements are necessary in this age of postmodernism, postbehaviorism, postlogical positivism. He wants to put the guts, the fortitude, the exhilaration back into education, and until you become used to his willingness to expose his own "scholarly pursuits and contemplations" in agonizingly human and persistently subjective terms, you may feel that you are reading a memoir or a fragment of autobiography. What you are witnessing, I think, is a religious man and a social scientist who is willing to take chances in establishing a more vibrant relationship with the studied environment. Thus, you will read his poems, be dared by his feelings, grapple with his intellect, sense the different angles from which he comes to a topic, and learn to believe in his humility.

In *Christ the Placenta* monolog becomes dialog. While you can but wonder how the Mentor would respond to these letters, you can hardly fail to respond yourself, at least to certain topics which the author introduces. One's own "scholarly pursuits and contemplations" get out on the table, face up, for reexamination and new commitment. The dialog cuts wide— through the social sciences and their relationship to the possibilities of transcendence in the world of human affairs; through the arts with their powers in the expression of leadership; through the sciences, potential new allies of religion; and through organizational management where the author is convinced transcendental experiences can be found, understood, and nurtured. David Bickimer asserts that "to be Christian is to be ecumenical," and for him the Spirit is Christ. Yet he knows that the Spirit already within each of us can be described in many ways, and expressed in even more, and it is the expression rather than the description that is the end of religious education.

R. BRUCE MCPHERSON
College of Education
University of Illinois of Chicago
May, 1982

Preface

EASTER SUNDAY MORNING
APRIL 11, 1982

DEAR JIM,

The Mystery of the Resurrection
The ultimate triumph—-
total transcendence.

It's very quiet this morning (3:00 A.M.), a good time to write this Preface, the first (i.e., Letter I) of the twelve letters that follow serves as an introduction, and the last (Letter XII) presents highlights of the other eleven. The overall thrust of the book is available to our readers, then, in both the first and last letter. But I think we are all so varied in our prehensive learning patterns that none should feel that such an initial overall grasp of the book's material is universally necessary. To some it may be, and it is available in Letters I and XII. To most, however, I suspect entering the sequence of letters at any point may be appropriate, trusting in the holonomic quality of the reality with which they deal. Just as *prehensively,* the whole is greater than the sum of its parts, holonomically, each part contains the whole. Such a "studied randomness" in approaching the book does two things. It allows the reader to engage in the kind of learning I experienced as I wrote the letters; it also opens up the book as one opens up an object of potential enjoyment. My greatest hope is that the book will be enjoyed.

1

Enjoyed . . . yes. Agreed with . . . no.

I am aware of the fact that the "unspoken" assumptions of much that is said here run counter to more than one articulated tenet of the world's organized religions. This fact prompts me to quickly claim total responsibility for the views herein, and to indicate that even colleagues and friends whom I cite by name are not to be assumed to be in agreement with me. Indeed, most of my colleagues and friends would not find such an agreement either comfortable or desirable. Therefore, when I, for example, in effect damn current bureaucracies, or suggest learning morals, including sexual morals, in the workplace, I do so on my own.

But while all responsibility is solely mine for the explorations and positions herein espoused, I still must thank many people for helping and encouraging me. First of these, in keeping totally consistent with the book's postulate of the teacher's primacy, are my own teachers. Including yourself, these include Sister Mary Bernadette, H.H.M., my first-grade teacher, a host of "Blue Nuns," an army of Jesuits, a Holy Cross contingent, a cohort of Sulpicians (remember Fr. Cuyler, S.S.?), and more than a few devout atheists. From all I have learned to learn prehensively and to share this gift with my own students.

After my teachers, I want to thank my students; from those at Cleveland East High School, who voted me "Teacher of the Century," to my students at Pace University. I can truly say that the content of these letters materialized as my own students supported me with patience, enthusiasm, understanding, honesty, love, and devotion to learning.

In all truth, much of what is contained in these letters occurred while I was actually engaged in that most hallowed and mysterious act of teaching. Perhaps most significant in this regard, because they were the most difficult, were the seminars at the New York City Board of Education. There I was able to test the viability of much of this book's meaning with mid-career educators coping daily with the debilitating effects of our massive bureaucracies' dysfunctions.

At Pace, also, the "family" feel and supportive ambience gave me the confidence to explore religion and education. Dean Fred Bunt and Dr. Leo Weitz gave me a New York home, not an easy thing to find. They, together with Dr. Carl Erdberg, Dr. Thomas Robinson, Dean Tony Bonaparte, Dr. Jack Schiff, and President Edward J. Mortola, took in and sustained a refugee from the corporate coups and bureaucratic boondoggles that go to make up much of life in the New York workplace. Without these gentlemen, this book would not exist.

Finally, at Pace, on a day-to-day basis Edith Gaal, our program assistant, was my life support system. A German Lutheran girl from Brooklyn, Edith constantly fed me "one liners" as I would share with her my thoughts about the book. The effect of these one-liners oftentimes was to have me re-think, rewrite, introduce, or eliminate . . . in effect, then, to edit on a day-to-day basis. Thanks to Edith, it is still true that "Close is not a cigar!" and "Self-praise stinks!"

As for my friends, they are mentioned throughout the letters. They are the "stuff" of my life and the constant source of energy for these letters. Mike and Paulette Racanelli and their wonderful family gave me a solid sense of "feet on the ground" even when I focused my own skepticism on myself, to much avail. David Kermani, Sal Viscardi, David Bruce Duncan, John Ashbery, Richard and Martha Chiriani, all gave me whatever poetic wings I have. It is to them that I owe the wonderful sense of interplay between art, poetry, science, music, etc., and religion.

Friends like Fr. Paul Byrnes are rare. More than friend, Paul

has been creative and patient confessor, consoler, and priest. Of him I once said in a poem: "Restorative soul savior
child-like belief saver."

The wonderful spirit of Jolanta Stankowski, who typed the manuscript, buoyed me through the final stages. The layout of many of the poems as they appear here, was originally designed by Rose Romero Rivera. Both Rose and Jo can create a work of art with paper and typewriter. Rose, in addition, saw that much of the poetry cried out for special arrangement on the page and quite intuitively typed the poetry *as art object.* How blessed can you be?

The Easter daffodils are beginning to droop. I talked to my oldest sister, Adele, in Cleveland and to my Aunt Lou who said she hoped she would understand this book. I told her understanding wasn't required as long as she believed.

And that brings me to the last few words I'll write. They are about belief. We are all awash on a constantly fluctuating sea of values unless we believe. For belief, not just truth, makes you free. If we are so graced, as we flounder in this value flux, we spot certain aspects of it all which reduce our anguish, terror, and despair. But spotting these aspects is one thing; they also require belief. Once we believe, we realize that our "environment" has a direction, knows where it's going, and supports us rather than aborts us. In this sense then, "Christ the placenta self-addressed-stamped envelopes the world."

YOURS IN THE AFTERBIRTH OF THE RESURRECTION,
DAVID
NEW YORK, CAIRO, DEEP CREEK LAKE, 1981–82

Letter I

> Better, you said, to stay
>   cowering
> Like this in the early lessons, since the promise of learning
> Is a delusion, and I agreed, adding that
> Tomorrow would alter the sense of what had already been
>   learned,
> That the learning process is extended in this way, so that
>   from this standpoint
> None of us ever graduates from college,
> For time is an emulsion, and probably thinking not to grow
> up
> Is the brightest kind of maturity for us, right now at any rate.

—John Ashbery

Dear Jim,

Ever since we agreed that I should write these letters to you, I have been filled with a certain sense of dread. If I knew what the dread was all about, I supposed it would disappear . . . or at least somehow be partially alleviated. But the feeling persists and so I think it only fair to point out that these letters are written by one who prefers to remain and in reality still is "cowering like this in the early lessons" to a significant extent. I am writing these letters constantly fighting the feeling

of dread of a coward, afraid to expose himself in all his igno-
rance, all his contradictions, and even, perhaps, all his imma-
ture contrariness. Truly, I write to you as one who knows that
"the promise of learning is a delusion," not in the sense that
anyone in the "early" or late lessons was being lied to or sold a
questionable bill of goods but in the sense that "the sense of
what has already been learned" is constantly up for grabs. This
fact is, all by itself, enough to confirm me in my cowardice.

A contract, however, is a contract and here are the promised
letters, fraught as I fear they will be with an inadequate grasp of
an everchanging landscape of thought and feeling, and rich I
am sure in contradictions and non sequiturs.

In this first letter to you, I'll proffer you my thanks (and
apologia for accepting), describe the nature of the task I have
set for myself, and discuss the methodology that I will use as I
proceed through the next months writing these letters to you.

THANK YOU (APOLOGIA)

First, I want to thank you for the invitation to write these
letters. That I am an unlikely recipient of such a request is
obvious not only to me, but also to those who have known me
to be other than a paragon of virtue. Moreover, my track record with my own organized-religious tradition (Roman Catholic) is of an on-again, off-again, ambivalent nature. As I indicated to you over dinner at Barbetta's restaurant here in New
York, in a curious way, sometimes the farther I get from overt
involvement with organized religion, the stronger my faith in
God becomes. In other words, it has on occasion been my
experience that, as I removed myself from the "pressures" of
organized religion, the easier and more readily did an act of
faith spring from my person.

How explain such a riddle? Some small explanation may, indeed, come from the nature of my personality and the nature of religion as it is bureaucratically delivered.

One of the most fascinating pieces of social science research I know speaks to the curvilinear relationship between stress and productivity. The research, as performed by Alan Brown is reported in the Getzels text on *Educational Administration as a Social Process*.[1] In effect, what Brown reports is that stress (i.e., ego-threatening pressures) when applied in a superordinate-subordinate relationship (in a situation where the superordinate is attempting to increase the productivity of the subordinate) can cause the action of the subordinate to deteriorate if that subordinate is a) above average in academic achievement, b) ambitious, and c) neurotic. On the other hand, if the subordinate is a) the average academic achiever, b) quite emotionally normal, and c) not all that ambitious, the application of stress will cause his or her performance to be enhanced.

My neuroses are not secret. My obsessive compulsive nature is a matter of medical, if not public, record. Then, too, my entrepreneurial spirit is rarely hidden under a bushel, and my academic record shows me to be no slouch in that regard. It seems that what I had been experiencing in my organized religious interactions—including religious education—was ego-threatening stress—e.g., threat of eternal damnation—and such an approach with a neurotic, academic, entrepreneur like myself was debilitating to the extent that the desired action (i.e., an act of faith) was impossible for me.

Let me hasten to add that I am deeply grateful for all the religious experiences, including religious education, I have had in my life. It may sound a bit inconsistent for me to attest to such gratitude, yet the fact is that God makes a diamond through great pressures. Faith is a diamond, and pressure is necessary up to a point. But the relationship is curvilinear. By that I mean that, up to a certain point, unique to each of us, pressure enhances the creation of faith. But beyond that point, it debilitates and crushes faith itself, especially of neurotic (creative?) ambitious, intellectuals.[2]

And so it seems to me that my removal from the organized pressures of religion was, in effect, a strategy which increased my faith.

One other point, in a somewhat similar vein, seems appropriate to make at this time. As no one is worthy of faith, so, too, no one is worthy of writing about education to faith. I certainly sense my own unworthiness to write about religious education. Yet, as this sense of unworthiness grows, the more I know that I am supposed to be writing these letters to you. I cannot help, however, but be concerned that those who have devoted their whole lives to religious instruction, like yourself, would think me a bit "cheeky" if not outright guilty of *chutzpah* for even attempting the task I am attempting. After all, neither my lifestyle nor my professional pursuits would seem to make me even mildly appropriate for such a task.

I can only respond to such a reaction—perfectly legitimate as it is—by saying that *all education is religious education*. Such is one of the basic assumptions of these letters. While I will have more to say on this subject in hopes of making it clearer and more acceptable, I feel it important to point out, at this juncture that the purpose of all education is to bring persons to a communion with something transcending themselves; just as Abraham Maslow points out that the purpose of management is the same. If this assumption sounds curious, then I accept the challenge to make it more palatable. If this assumption sounds destructive of time-honored distinctions between and among fields of human endeavor, then I must plead guilty. The existential "melding" of science and religion which is emerging in literature of all types was predicted back in the thirties by Teilhard de Chardin and others. It is necessarily having its practical implications in our day-to-day professional life. If fields once so apparently distinct as science and religion are now being seen in some unifying megatheory, then how much greater must be the conversion of motifs, methodologies, assumptions, etc. between and among practical "disciplines" of the same genus with only specific difference—i.e., secular and religious education?

All of this is not to say that in every context secular education *is* religious education. The operational details of both fields make for ready and easy operational distinctions. But it seems a misreading of Western culture to draw a hard-and-fast line between the two areas of instruction.

MY TASK

The religious nature of secular education in the West may perhaps become clearer as I endeavor to spell out the exact nature of the task of these letters. Simply stated, my purpose is to urge that *the focus of religious education be the facilitation of the acquisition of mystic states on the part of the religious learner.* Because of the nature of my own professional career, I choose to suggest ways that this goal can be obtained which may seem to differ somewhat from the "traditional." I certainly would not argue with anyone else who, while granting that mystical experience is the ultimate objective of religious instruction, maintained that a most effective and efficient way to go about doing this is the study of scripture, tradition, sacred texts, commentaries, etc. Indeed, it is my current personal experience that such is often the case for me. But such is not always the case, and my own hegira seems to have been immersed in social science, the arts, and to a lesser but growing extent, the physical and biological sciences. And so the suggestions I will offer religious educators will spring from my own experiences in these three areas of activity. I will, of course, use sacred texts, etc., but I do so bereft of any credentials as to my prowess in their use and interpretation per se. And in a sense I will argue for their use, not alone, but in *tandem* with the intellectual and aesthetic contributions of our era.

As I review my purpose and my suggestions, however, it becomes clear to me and I hope to you that my purpose and my suggested methods and "materials" are not very different from those of Plato. Certainly, in Plato one can be a philosopher-king only after the visionary experience of the blinding light of the "One." And to bring the student to this vision, Plato used mathematics, astronomy, the science and arts of his day. So, you see, at the very Platonic foundations of Western education we can find similar purpose and materials which I am suggesting for religious educators of today. It is in this light that I suggest that all education, conceived in the Platonic manner, is religious education. Is not Plato's vision of the "one" a union with God, an illusion-transcending experience? The acquisition of a mystic state rests at the core of Western education. Then, too, the very root meaning of the word "education," if we are to avoid the denigrating effects of what Paulo Friere calls the "banking" concept of education" is the "leading out of." That is to say, that at the basis of Western education is the observation that all knowledge is contained within the individual ("the kingdom of God is within you"). And the process of education is simply a matter of bringing the student to this self-realization.

Even the word *religious* has a similar root meaning. For it means a "*tying* back up," a "reuniting"—that is, something is *religious* if it takes the loose ends of our spiritual awareness and unifies them back once again into the unity, the oneness, of the universal being.[3]

What I am saying here is that even when root meanings of words are considered the two words *religious* and *education* seem to be pointing in the same direction. The former seeks to put everything back where it came from and to lock it in there (i.e., union with God, the universal consciousness, the "one"), while the latter seeks to make us recall where we all came from and ultimately to bring us to an awareness of our "communion" with the totality of existence, the "one."

I will have more to say about this in the next letter, which deals with the nature of the mystical experience from an educational point of view. I hope I have provided enough insight at this point to allow the argument to proceed.

MY METHOD

Methodologically, as you suggested, the letters will be a mixture of my own experiences in social science, the arts, and the physical and biological sciences and my own transcendental experiences reported through the poetry I have written in an effort to capture the meaning and beauty of the experiences. Further, the book is in letter form; the letter format seems important because of its personal nature. And if there is one thing religious education must be, it is *personal*.

Moreover, the letter format seems most conducive to capturing the flavor of a "naturalistic inquiry technique" which I plan to use in the pursuit of my goal. Naturalistic inquiry, as I see it, rests somewhere between highly subjective opinionizing and cool, calculating, objective, scientific observing. Actually, I like to think of my method in those letters as a sort of "poetic scientism" which, like contemporary visual and language arts, often seeks to encapsulate into its ruminations and findings the content of the surrounding environment. Thus, while I do report on my own experiences in scholarly pursuit and in contemplation, I do so utilizing the reports of others in their own scholarly pursuits and contemplations. Naturalistic inquiry seeks to foster this reaching out of investigator to investigator so that each may balance the other off, saving the reader from egregious, self-seeking subjectivism as well as heartless, dispassionate, almost inhuman scientific detachment.[4]

This last point is worth a bit more discussion. When push comes to shove, one of the basic reasons for my writing these letters to is encourage others to do the same. By others, I mean other *teachers*. I am writing these letters as a teacher; not as a scientist, not as a manager, not as a consultant, not as an editor, etc., but as a *teacher*. The reason I want to stress this point is that being a teacher today, at least in my experience, means being ignored, easily dismissed, and even looked down on.

The most important career in the world is that of *teacher*. As far as I am concerned, to be a teacher is to have, quite literally, a divine calling . . . i.e., a vocation. Teachers today, alas, are surrounded by and at the mercy of people who either do not know this or do not care. But whether or not bureaucrats and politicians know it, teaching is a sacred act, intensely personal, and basically mystical in its essence. Whitehead knew that teaching and learning were essentially religious processes. This religious essence of teaching is what I hope these letters will elucidate from one teacher's experience. And if I am successful, other teachers will join me in writing similar letters so that we can share, in a very personal way, our mutual but unique experience of the divine essence of teaching.

It would not surprise me if some, coming from within or without the more traditional approaches to religious education, would view these letters as a vulgarization, even a secularization of the religious experience of a teacher. Such an observation springs from a dichotomous form of thinking which, it seems to me, cannot hope to match the phenomenon at hand.

But what is more, even if the observation is construed as accurate, it cannot detract from my own experience of the sacred nature of that in which I engage myself. While others may see it as profane, my own immersion in education deserves testimony to its genuinely transcendental nature. And even if these letters should really simply document the personal "delusions" of a teacher, they still can be seen as documentation of a teacher believing in and relishing the wonderful possibility of a heaven, even here on earth. The point is that these letters need not be considered evidence of genuine "religious experience." All they need to be considered is evidence of a *teaching mind* experiencing the promise of learning and sharing that promise with students.[5]

And so my purpose is to encourage religious educators to bring their students to direct experience of the eternal. I suggest they can do this by utilizing social science, the arts, and the physical and biological sciences. My suggestions take the form of personal letters elaborating on my own naturalistic inquiry into the issues at hand. The letters draw on scholarly output and contemplative products of other-like investigators as well as my own. Incidentally, these investigators furnish a welcome balance to my own ever-present Christianity for they are ecumenical in nature. To me, to be a Christian is to be ecumenical and my equating of secular and religious education opens us the field beyond ecumenicism for a plethora of "peak" mystical experience drawn from a variety of sources. As I'll try to show, from Humpty Dumpty to Arjuna, from Kubrick to Mohammed, the transcendent state is there to study and hopefully to emulate.

While these letters will progress like all other letters, I think it possible to predict the major topic and thrust of each. As I envision the progression, the following lineup of subjects seems probable.

    I.   Purpose and method
   II.   The nature of the mystical experience ecumenically considered
  III.   The social sciences and the transcendent state
  IV.   Implications of the social sciences and the transcendent state for religious education
   V.   The arts and the transcendent state
  VI.   Implications of the arts and the transcendent state for religious education
 VII.   The physical sciences and the transcendent state
VIII.   Implications of the physical sciences and the transcendent state for religious education
  IX.   Some unsolved problem areas:
         —Organized religious authority and the religious education teacher
         —Sexuality and the sexual revolution and the religious education teacher
         —The Moral Majority and the religious education teacher
         —Organizing the delivery of religious education
         —The interface between religious and secular education
   X.   Conclusions[6]

Having presented this tentative lineup of "events to come" via these letters, it's time to end this first letter to you. I think I'll do so with a brief commentary on the title of this book. The phrase "Christ the placenta" comes from a poem I wrote some time ago, early in one of my "returns" to organized worship.

Here it is in its totality.

Canto for a Summer Sunday in Ordinary Time

There is no end
to what we can do
and where we can go
together
We'll turn hell into heaven
with Paolo and Francesca
joining Francis and Dominic
making Dante's downs ups
at last no false ethic
enjoined on man

Christ the placenta
self-addressed-stamped
envelopes the world
embryo
sweetly curled in fetal form
eyesopen I watch and breathe
his sustaining liquids
lavers of love and support
nourishing and pacifying
me patiently waiting
on a wonderfully long summer's day in the city
hot but so bearable because you bring the
sundown apocalyptically protecting me from
it and the end of the world.

The first part of this poem speaks to an experience of the
unity of opposites. It "boasts" that we have the potential to
turn the opposite of heaven (i.e., hell) into heaven in such a
way that even Dante's illicit lovers (Paulo and Francesca) will
be seen as inhabiting the same eternal abode as two founders

of celibate religious orders. While I must confess to sympathy for the plight of the illicit lovers and even an aversion for Dante's judgment of them (who's to judge?), I think that neither the sympathy nor the aversion are at issue in these lines. Rather the impact of the hyperbole is to underscore the fact that we do not have to rest content with the way things appear to us to be. In other words, things are not only not as they appear, they are not what they could and should be. We have all within us the wherewithal to transcend this day-to-day experience . . . for we come from and we return to a transcendental plane where opposites meet.

Through "Christ the Placenta" we are nourished and protected on our journey. I wrote this poem after seeing Stanley Kubrick's *2001* and before seeing Nicolas Roeg's *The Man Who Fell to Earth,* both films about the arrival (from another land) of "strangers" to the earth.[7] The conclusion of *2001* has a wide-eyed embryo floating through space in a life-giving placenta, in effect its spaceship. In *The Man Who Fell to Earth* the same theme appears. An individual comes to earth leaving behind another kind of existence.

We have all fallen to earth and someday, unlike the ill-fated Humpty Dumpty, we'll get back together again . . . i.e., return whence we came. The difference between Kubrick and Roeg is in the presence of the placenta provided for the voyager pilgrim.

In the last line of the poem, "it and the end of the world," I allude to the imminent end of the world which seems to be a large part of my thinking and of many people I know. I am told, for example, that it is a topic of great interest at cocktail parties of scientists who seem to be expecting the final cataclysm. Now, I have no problem with these "doomsday" types except in their negativism toward the final event. To be honest, I feel that the end of the world comes to each of us individually, no matter what else happens. And I do believe that in the "end" of each one of us, Christ will be there in his return in a most supportive, placenta-like fashion. Indeed, Christ . . . in the images of the poem . . . will envelop the whole world and, being self-addressed and even self-stamped, he will return it and us with him back whence we came, to the "one," to his father.

And so the coalescense of extreme opposites in one prepares the way for the human soul to grasp its ultimate destiny back in the wholeness of being from which it came. We can grow in our realization of this fact and transcend the agony and pain of daily existence if only for an instant.

The essence of the experience is reunion with our source, our font or ground of being. In short, we all are meant to return to the kingdom and the return is, *unlike* Plato's union with the "one," available to and possible for all of us. For the kingdom is "within" us, if we would but know it always. My roots lead me to call the sustainer of this process of return, the nourisher of this spiritual appetite—Christ.

Finally, with reference to the title, as far as your being my *mentor,* such is the case and I have always cherished that fact. When you met me in your seminars at Notre Dame in the '60s, you met a rigid, conservative incarnation of the *ratio studiorum.* The "revolution" which you enabled me to effect in my life, not only in seminar, but also in long personal discussions, and your expressions of Christian charity have stayed with me through all these years. Today they still serve as a model for me in my relationship with *my* students, a model I too often fail to emulate.

It's the birthday of the Virgin (she'll be 2000 years old next year, in Christian time), Rosh Hashanah is upon us, Ramaden has passed and "Christ the placenta self-addressed-stamped envelopes the world."

WITH GRATITUDE AND LOVE,
DAVID

Notes to Letter I

1. Alan F. Brown, "The Differential Effect of Stress-Inducing Supervision on Classroom Teaching Behavior," Doctoral Dissertation, University of Alberta, 1961 in Jacob W. Getzels, James M. Lipham, and Roald F. Campbell, *Educational Administration As A Social Process: Theory, Research, Practice* (New York: Harper & Row, 1968), pp. 270–280.

2. I realize that I can be accused here of blowing a rather small and limited study of stress and personality way out of proportion. Yet, since I have been dealing on a regular basis these days with "burnt-out" teachers the relevance of this little research "gem" comes back at me time and time again. For the burn-outs I deal with are inevitably the above-average academic types, almost as neurotic as I am—their neuroses vent themselves in creativity when given the opportunity—who have been the real producers in our classrooms. They are ambitious types whose response to the growing monolithic Weberian bureaucracy within which they are asked to thrive has been debilitated productivity and, ultimately, loss of self-esteem leading to burn-out.

Given this experience, my conclusion, in light of Brown's study, is that the bureaucracies we deal with are in and of themselves stressful. Given this fact, we can anticipate that—and this surfaces in much research—these bureaucracies will abort the elite, stifle the creative and reward the mediocre.

The exact nature of the stressful dynamics is not hard to delineate. These "burned out cases" are the professionals in our midst for whom the canons of behavior revolve solely around the uniqueness of the individual case and whose criterion for success is "the cure." On the other hand, in a necessarily stressful way, the canons of the bureaucrat vouchsafe that individuals are but cogs in the wheel, and the criterion for effectiveness is certainly not the cure, but, rather, *fulfilling procedures.* This bureaucratic "ethic" is the "killer" when one investigates the demise of creative individuals in our large organizations. Aside from the fact that the type of individual who can thrive on such a wheel-cog mentality may be more than flirting with sociopathology, the bureaucratic practices alone are, of their very nature, ego-threatening and foster "productivity" on the part of the mediocre, lack-luster figure whose performance is enhanced by "applying the screws." Apply those same bureaucratic screws to the bright, creative ambitious individual and you witness the death of that individual. Either he or she is aborted or burns out, or—and here is perhaps the tragedy—the individual experiences moral debilitation to the point of character deterioration, finds himself or herself with no inner sense of right or wrong, and accordingly proceeds to go through a career solely out of survival motivation in a tour de force of unprincipled manipulation of perceptions. Hence the brood-of-vipers syndrome, no stranger to secular or ecclesiastic, highly structured organizations now and in the past.

3. William Irwin Thompson, *The Time Falling Bodies Take to Light: Mythology, Sexuality and the Origins of Culture,* (New York: St. Martin's Press, 1981.) This book is fascinating in its modern translation of the eternal verities of all religions. I cite it here because it helped to focus my own thinking on the best way to define religion for my purpose in these letters. The definition I use seems to permeate Thomson's treatise.

4. Fritjof Capra, *The Tao of Physics,* (New York: Bantam Books, 1980). Gary Zukav, *The Dancing Wu Li Masters: An Overview of the New Physics,* (New York: Bantam Books, 1980). In a later letter on science and religious education, an argument for this "naturalistic inquiry" will be implicit in as much as, according to the two works cited in this footnote, the model of the separate observer objectively observing a universe quite apart from himself or herself may have been a figment of our imagination. If I correctly understand our

scientific colleagues who have emerged somewhat shaken from their would-be objective observations of high-energy, particle experiments, a better description of the "scientific" observer might well be that of *participant observer*. In other words, the interaction of observer and observed is such in quantum physics that one cannot speak of the relationship in terms of the "old" scientist vis-à-vis external reality model. In this light, a less dispassionate mode of inquiry on our part here may not be all that unscientific. Indeed, in looking to convey their findings, some quantum physicists have discovered the language of Buddhism and Hinduism useful. In other words, the former seeming irrelevance of mytho-poetic, subjective forms of expression common to religion, has faded, in some physicists minds, in light of the co-relevance of Western science and Eastern mysticism. Apparently, even scientists have discovered a weakness in "almost inhuman scientific detachment."

5. Robert J. Starratt, "Teacher in the Promised Land", *National Elementary Principal* LVIII, 4 (January, 1979), pp. 12–17. I am really indebted to Jerry Starratt, not only for the article in question but for our conversations about teaching and what the promised land has to do with that. If nothing else, his thinking has enabled me to reset my own sights on what it means for me to be a teacher. But, more than that, his type of thinking on teaching enables me to accept my own weaknesses and still go on teaching. For as he is quick to point out, even if one finds oneself not living in the promised land, that does not mean that one does not believe in one. Indeed, it is this very belief that things can be better, not the fact that they are now or even will be in the very near future, that is the moral well-spring which enables every teacher to stand up and be a witness for the better world to come.

6. Actually, the book came out to be twelve letters. The lineup of events is basically as projected in this original list, but Letter V in the original list ("The Arts and the Transcendent State") is Letter VI, Letter VI is Letter VII, Letter VII is Letter VIII, and Letter VIII is Letter IX. This "mixup" happened because of a junket to Cairo as witnessed in a new, unprojected letter, Letter V. Then, the projected Letter IX ("Some Unsolved Problem Areas") becomes Letter XI because of the

special "Extra" Letter X in the actual book which explains the haitus between letters. The addition of two "extra" letters, then, brings the total number of letters to twelve with the projected Letter X becoming the actual Letter XII ("Conclusions"). A special poetry section, "Excerpts from The Apperceptive Mass," is inserted between Letter IX and X.

7. Thompson, *The Time Falling Bodies Take to Light,* pp. 9, 34–37. Inspiration for a poem about transcendence from the movies seems less unlikely in light of Thomson's observation about the opportunity such science fiction films provide the scientific mind to experience the mythopoetic view of the universe, a view Thomson is much enamored of and which I think can well describe the mind of a teacher brokering the blandishments of the "fallen world" to his or her students while proffering the existence of a better way to be which does not rely on these blandishments. Incidentally, Thomson's treatment of myth, religion, and sex is fascinating. His emphasis on the female dimension of the spiritual life should come as good news to those who seek a better balance between the male and female aspects of our existence.

Letter II

Dear Jim,

Happy New Year! I am deliberately writing this letter to you on this day because it was one year ago, on Rosh Hashana, that I experienced what is, to date, my own peak "peak experience" (to use Maslow's term). But before I go into detail on that experience, as promised, I would like to discuss the nature of these peak or transcendental experiences as we see them in this late twentieth century. And I thought I would begin the discussion with a recounting of an episode in which you figured most predominately in the days we shared at Notre Dame. It has a lot to do with the meeting of students' needs, an activity at which you excel.

Meeting Needs

As you will recall, I was suffering one of my notorious backaches, the reality of which was often suspect in the eyes of my peers, and the causes of which were more legendary than real in the eyes of those who perceived me as living out Hugh Hefner's paradigm of the successful young male. I hasten to add that both the perceivers and Mr. Hefner's paradigm were equally erroneous . . . at least in my case. At any rate, on the

22

occasion of one of these backaches, you brought the entire seminar to my little house on Saint Peter's Street in South Bend, Indiana. It was a highly successful session, as I recall, and this one episode was just one of many similar instances in a memorable educative experience for me.

The point of this recollection is that you were ever ready to adjust your instruction to meet the needs of those enrolled. And while many would (and did) accuse you of extremes, it was this constant "meeting of needs" that made your own version of religious education extremely effective and efficient.

Religious instruction, as I see it, must be designed to meet the needs of the learner. But why is this so? And precisely what are these needs? Can it truly be said that every rabbi, every Sunday School teacher, every nun, etc., must meet the learners' needs before he or she can achieve success in religious instruction? If the answer to this question is yes, then a solid sense of what these needs are will be necessary for success.

At this point in the discussion it seems necessary to posit two working hypotheses. The first of these working hypotheses is that any learner, in as much as he or she is a learner, is a "less than fully socialized worker." This curious phrase is of Dan Lortie's making and is found in his relatively recent treatise, *School Teacher*.[1] By way of explanation and application of Lortie's thinking to our task, I am positing that any learner is, in effect, undergoing a task-oriented process which, upon successful completion, will render that learner-worker socialized. While in the learning situation, however, the learner is, relative to the task at hand, heuristically considered to be a *partially* socialized worker.

Viewed in this light, then, the religious education learner is subject to the same laws that operate in the workplace. On the basis of this working hypothesis, then, much of the scientific work I bring to bear on the religious education scene will come from social science research done on the workplace and the management thereof. I hope this hypothesis does not constitute too great a leap for the reader at this time. I hope to justify it as best as I can as we proceed.

Granted the hypothesis, however, we can now feel free to borrow from some very classic studies of human motivation; studies designed, for example, to help Harvard and the business community discover the "secrets" of increased productivity—studies which, granted the hypothesis, will permit us to explore increased effectiveness and efficiency in religious instruction utilizing a long history of social science theory and research. I am referring, of course, to Roethlisberger and Dickson's *Management and the Worker* and all its concomitant and subsequent hegemony in the study of the workplace.

Furthermore, granted this hypothesis, and building on the results of the theory and research just mentioned, we can point to a probable conclusion of these letters at this early point. That conclusion is that, if religious education is to be effective and efficient, and if the needs of the workers and learners must be met to make religious education effective and efficient, then the strategic task for those who are responsible for planning, developing, and managing, religious instruction is to meet the *needs of the religious education teachers.* For if we consider the learner in religious education to be a partially socialized worker, then we must consider, a fortiori, the teacher to be the worker per se; and, as we shall see, it is the worker whose own needs are met who is most effective and efficient. Simply put, if we desire effective and efficient religious education, then we must meet the needs of the religious education teachers, for only in this way will this individual teacher-worker be increasingly effective and efficient in meeting the needs of the learner-worker.

THE NATURE OF NEEDS TO BE MET

A second working hypothesis of import at this point has to do with the nature of the needs which have been the focus of the discussion immediately above. What are these needs and how have they been determined? Another "leap" for the reader is required at this juncture. Our working hypothesis about these needs is that ultimately at the crest of all the needs of humans is the need for mystical experience.

While you might say that this working hypothesis is not common knowledge, I promise to demonstrate that it is not unfounded in a significant body of theory and research. Moreover, it is a need that has been systematically "isolated" and investigated in a field notorious for its here-and-now, day-to-day, nuts-and-bolts pragmatism: a world seemingly crassly materialistic and self-interested. I am speaking once again of the field of management science and worker motivation.[2]

According to this second working hypothesis, then, each learner in a religious education setting has the need to transcend the here and now, to "peak out" so to speak, i.e., to experience an altered state of consciousness such that he or she experiences "communion" with the ultimate reality from whence and to whence we all, pilgrimlike, proceed.

In these letters, then, we will consider the learner a partially socialized worker in the religious education setting and the teacher as *the* worker in the religious setting. We will further consider that for both to be effective and efficient (increasingly so) their needs must be met. Further, we shall consider the rock-bottom (i.e., ultimate) need for both teacher and learner to be the need for transcendental experience. With these two working hypotheses articulated we can then proceed on to the topic of this letter, i.e., the nature of the transcendental experience.

A PERSONAL "CASE STUDY"

While it is true that the Cabbalah cautions against telling too much of one's own experience of the "mysteries" if only for economy-of-energy reasons, I am prompted to share with you at this point what amounts to my peak "peak experience" to date. I do so to provide a personal, contemporary "case study" of exactly what I am talking about when I use the phrase "transcendental experience." I'll introduce it with an excerpt from the poem I wrote about it. Before I present the poem, however, you might be interested in a few of the details surrounding its writing.[3]

While I wrote the poem, "The Swansong of Gloria Glimpse," to "record" the "peak experience" in question, it is dedicated to David Bruce Duncan, a thriving collage-painter here in New York and a good friend of mine. I am considering buying his most recent work entitled "Holy Family." I would like you to see it, if only because David has already said we could use it for the cover of this book if you like it. "Holy Family" will figure in a later letter so perhaps it might well be considered for inclusion in some way or other.[4]

Actually, I wrote the poem *for* David because, in this instance at least, our heads seemed to be amazingly close regarding the creation of the poem. By that, I mean to say that I am not sure who made up the title. The title is a slightly veiled, humorous reference to a meeting David had with Gloria Swanson which he was telling me about as I was trying to tell him about my own "glorious glimpse" at Mass. The words of the title seemed to tumble from our mouths simultaneously so that I don't know who should get the "credit." David's own religiosity is very deep.

David is, then, the inspiration for the repeated references and allusions to collage-painting throughout the poem, and I doubt if I would have found an appropriate vehicle for the thoughts of the poem if it hadn't been for him.[5]

THE SWANSONG OF GLORIA GLIMPSE
for David Bruce Duncan

See the pope and see the pap-
acy . . . . ah see
pole pope decline recline
in western dying efficacy
see the whole
forget the rhyme
layed papers reflecting
layered lights
assume the attitude
of gesso, lacquer
porous smooth foundation
of new truth
On Roshoshon did poet praying
in chapel simply
bend knee and worship
and simple priests hands
raised for sacred momentum
accompanied
    —veil lifted
    —insight real
    —disco in fishbowl
    —ultimate non-vision
    —apophatic excellence
    —vale pierced
    —wonder wrought
next door for want of caring
the perfect Byzantine church
declined but not deterioriated

> awaiting the rehabilitation
> of the attitude to be assumed
> human again once aware of
> the promise
> That's all it was the new years day
> a simple announcement
> a glorious glimpse
> gloria gloria gloria gloria
> in a glimpse us
> redeemed is seen
> through suffering artists
> with clothes
> rent unseamed
> the veil is rent
> to pay the lord of the land
> seemed easy

While I wrote this poem before I ever thought of doing this book, I think that we can look at it and begin to see some of the characteristics of peak experiences. In this way we can build to a better picture of what we are talking about as being the object of religious education.

Curiously, the line "disco in fishbowl" occurred to me at about the same time, unbeknownst to me, John Ashbery's "Litany"[6] was being published with its reference to our human existence occurring in a watery fishbowl. John, a uniquely fine friend and poet, and I seem to agree that human vision on a day-to-day basis is very limited . . . as if we were in a fishbowl. The fishbowl is the equivalent of Paul's "darkling glass." The truth alluded to comes clearly into sight when a "peak experience" occurs giving us a glorious glimpse beyond the mirror, beyond the fishbowl, on into the sacred heart of reality.

It seems to me that the purpose of religious education in any faith is to increase the possibility for the achievement of this transcendental state of mind on the part of the learner. That is to say the ultimate in religious experience is the achieving of this state of mind. It is the achieving of this state here, or if not here, in the next life, that is the object of leading "the good life," doing good works, and worshiping God . . . . the object of religious education.

The lines

> "after just one sober glimpse
> can one change one's whole life"

speak to a characteristic of the transcendental experience which is universally reported. Peter Fingesten, chairman of the Art and Humanities Department at Pace University is quick to recount an experience he had in his teens. Near death, he suddenly pierced the veil and saw the ultimate reality, an experience which still today, as I understand it, years later, fashions and shapes his entire career and lifestyle. In his "The 'Core-Religious' or 'Transcendent,' Experience," Abraham Maslow addresses himself to this characteristic of the mystical, ecstatic occurrence. The experience is so intense as to become a hub around which the wheel of one's life can easily and effectively revolve.[7]

Another characteristic which other scientists note about the experience is the ineffability thereof. At the same time, they note that those who have the experience often spend the rest of their lives doing everything possible to describe the event and encourage others to pursue the same. Thus, while the following lines from the poem are an effort to document and describe the experience which occurred as my local priest raised his left hand over the chalice at the time of consecration at a Mass on

Rosh Hashana, 1979, they must ultimately be considered a weak representation of the actual event.

> —veil lifted
> —insight real
> —disco in fishbowl
> —ultimate non-vision

In detail

veil lifted:
    The removal of the veil of illusion which surrounds us
insight real:
    an experience of confrontation with ultimate reality
disco in fishbowl:
    As I indicated before, a feeling that the "fishbowl" of life has suddenly been seen as just that and that, beyond the fishbowl was a brilliant white light quite inadequately presented her as the strobes and mirror-speckled, granular, brilliance of a disco (disco, of course, means *I learn* in Latin).
ultimate non-vision:
    When the experience occurred, I did not look up (as I had in the past) for the reality to be experienced was much more real than that which could be seen. There was no need to move a muscle.
apophatic excellence:
    truly there is no way that this experience can be adequately described, which makes it excellent material to be described *apophatically*—i.e., it was *not* to be seen.
wonder wrought:
    The attitude in which I discovered myself was that of

awe, wonder, and basically devout, adoring
conversation.
vale pierced:
   A reference to this "vale of tears" in which we live and
   the fact that the experience was one of peace and joy
   dissipating all tearful sadness.

This very personal presentation of what I mean by transcendent experience is proffered as a case study of what I am getting at when I say such an experience is the object of religious education. But you don't have to rely on me for such case studies. The history of the world is rife with them and, in order to further clarify the nature of the experience, I thought it would be best now to review a small sample of such experiences as we know them from the past. In so doing it is my hope that the nature of the experience will become clear and that the ecumenical nature of the experience and those who experience them will be evident. With that in mind, then, let's begin with what I consider to be the theoretical underpinning of all Western education, Plato's cave.[8]

SOME HISTORY

The experience of transcendence is spoken of these days as being accessible by all, possible for all, and highly individualized in its mode of arrival. Let me quickly point out, however, that all these characteristics were not apparent throughout all of history. For Plato himself can be interpreted as reserving this experience to the would-be, future philosopher kings. Nevertheless, this transcendent experience is the experience of the "good" which Plato reports. The seventh book of *The Republic* with its magnificent treatise on "The

Cave" is basically a treatise on the acquisition and the after-math of the acquisition of such a transcendental state.

In "The Cave," as readers we watch one captive's journey upon his being freed from the fetters which heretofore have locked his vision on the wall and the shadowy moving "ob-jects" thereon. Upon release from his chains, he ultimately discovers the light which is causing the statues, carried in front of it by unseen bearers, to cast their shadow on the wall where they, the shadows, are mistaken for real "objects" by those still in fetters. In essence, this freed captive "transcends" the here-and-now, day-to-day illusion, observes the eternal light of truth, and returns to what is now clearly seen as illusion. We even watch as he stumbles to get his bearings after experienc-ing the real for the first time, in need of his peers sup-port . . . although they will think him mad.

But such an experience is not reserved for Plato and his followers. The Hindus have observed and preserved for us the experience of Arjuna on the battlefield:

> Suppose a thousand suns should rise together into the sky: such is the glory of the shape of God.

> Then the son of Pandu beheld the entire universe in all its multitudinous diversity, lodged as one being within the body of the God of gods.[9]

Buddhists experience *Nirvana*—and as Geoffrey Parinder argues in *Mysticism in the World's Religions*[10]—this state in many instances is clearly a mystic state in which the "unity" of all things is seen. Parinder is also helpful in detailing Jewish transcendental experience (it being Rosh Hashana, and all that) especially in the Cabalist and Hassidic (e.g., Martin Buber, "I-thou") schools. The Islamic Sufis and the Shiites of Iran are other examples of "mystics" who like Hallaj can say:

> I have become he whom I love and he has become myself
> We are two spirits in one body
> When you see me you see him.

Christians have Christ's testimony as to his own experience in John XIV when Christ replies to Thomas:

> If you had known me, you would have known my Father. And henceforth you do know him, and you have seen him.

and in Christ's reply to Philip:

> Philip, he who sees me sees the father.

In his book Parinder is also quick to point out that the arts in Christian lands are deeply imbued with this transcendent state of consciousness, a point to which we will return in a later letter.

The above section presents examples and an explanation of that which we seek as the end of all religious education. There can be no obvious ommissions to the listing because it does not pretend to even scratch the surface. Sacred and secular texts are filled with these accounts and further explication of the state we all seek is easily available from the poems of John of the Cross to *The Cloud of the Unknowing*. I hope I have clarified what I mean by my objective. I can finish this letter, then, with a brief foray into the sociological setting in which these letters will be published.

THE SOCIOLOGICAL SETTING

I am sure that someone versed in the sociology of religion will find (in what I have said so far) that I am just a creature of my time. Indeed, as I began my investigation I confess to having been totally unaware of the "timeliness" of this formulation. The interest I have encountered in this approach to religious education has been almost universal. What's more, the interest comes from sources I would have heretofore considered somewhat unlikely.

Young people, especially, have responded with nothing but encouragement. I can't meet with George Mederos (for example) our young co-director at the Uptown YMCA (of which I am chair) without his reminding me of this book and the need he sees for it. Artists like Richard Chiriani and scientists like his wife Martha have engaged me in intense conversations indicating to me that religious education viewed in this way was a "hot topic." Indeed, I am now convinced that I am surrounded by a world filled with an increasing number of individuals who quite consciously seek, in one form or another, the transcendent mental state. Some do through prayer, some through drugs, some through alcohol, some through jogging, some through throwing a pot on a wheel, some through writing poetry . . . all with varying degrees of results.

Why this universal interest in transcendence? I can only offer my own interpretation of the reason for this interest. The reason seems to have something to do with the omnipresence of spirit-crushing bureaucracies and monolithic corporations. In spite of all the so-called good aspects of these "organizations," their primary effect seems to be a deadening of the human will to create, a killing of the "Christ" (in Gibran's universal sense of the word) in all of us. To quote Hopkins in "God's Grandeur": "All is seared with trade." This organization crunch of the human spirit can be found from our educational systems to our ecclesiastical hierarchies, from our giant corporations to our public services administrations. The human spirit is then crushed. God is therefore dead . . . not in and of himself, but in man's eyes which have gone blind with the death of the soul, the advent of Eliot's "hollow men."

But nevertheless, the human spirit, like God's grandeur, will, according to Hopkins:

> . . . flame out like the shining from shook foil:
> it gathers to a greatness . . .

I guess what I am saying is that, whereas perhaps in previous times we could count on our institutions to help us achieve transcendence, more and more of us are thrust back on our own resources. Luckily, we have found within ourselves (many of us through heretofore unorthodox means) the ultimate resource, the "kingdom" of God within us, the experience of which, perhaps just once in this life or perhaps just promised in the next, is enough to make life worth living.

If anyone reads this as a negative readout on our institutionalized life across the board, he or she is reading it correctly. Exceptions to the rule are few and far between, to the extent that Chris Argyris has noted that the mature individual cannot exist today in most large organizations.[11] If we define mature as "hovering on the edge of meeting the need for transcendence," then we can see the problem. It is almost as if the worst of logical positivism has been incarnated in our institutions to the detriment of individual freedom and emotional satisfaction.

A study of institutional research has pointed out to me that the "crushing of the individual" by the institution goes hand in hand with lowered productivity and efficiency. And we can expect more of the same as long as we as individuals are forced to seek for transcendence, not in our formal cooperative efforts and in our organized work experiences, but almost, as it were, on our own, joined perhaps by a few other stubborn stalwarts who insist on achieving the heights of the spiritual experience.

And it is precisely this institutional research we will be concerned with in the next two letters. For this is the social science research we will bring to bear on a deeper understanding of religious education and the practical implications which this research has for the increased effectiveness and efficiency thereof. By way of propaedeutic, a quote from Maslow's *Eupsychian Management* is fitting. "We must ultimately assume at the highest theoretical level levels of Eupsychian theory a preference or a tendency to identify with more and more of the world, moving toward the ultimate of mysticism, a fusion with the world, or peak experience, cosmic consiousness."[12]

From your lips to God's ears, Abe!

AS EVER,
DAVID

Notes to Letter II

1. Daniel Lortie, *School Teacher: A Sociological Analysis*, (Chicago: University of Chicago Press, 1972), p. 138.

2. The notion that a "mystical experience" lies at the heart of sound management strikes my students, at first, as "hogwash" . . . . to quote one of them who seems to own a disco, a plantation, and other various and sundry enterprises. Still, as we see in the discussion of Plato's cave which follows, it should not seem so surprising. For my readings of "The Cave" in relationship to Plato's educational purpose leads me to the conclusion that "The Cave" is indeed an integral part of a very early management treatise . . . i.e., part of Plato's education "platform" designed to produce the managers of his day, often referred to as "philosopher-kings." The tran-

scendental aspects of the cave are very much at home in the production of future administrators and leaders as far as Plato was concerned.

Once having arrived at this conclusion, one wonders how this centrality of "transcendence" for government got lost in Western culture. Curiously, the loss of transcendence may have resulted from the West's prolonged religious aversion to empirical science. As luck would have it, it seems possible to concentrate on the spirit side of the "spirit-matter" duality and thereby miss the "unity" behind the duality, which unity is grasped only intuitively, "mystically," using the right side of the brain, so to speak.

I'll try to show that some top theorists, at least, have not lost the original Platonic message, i.e., Barnard and Maslow.

3. Having overcome my reluctance to proceeding in this personal way, I think I ought to point out that the occurence of transcendental experiences is commonplace and, so to speak, nothing to write home about. Indeed, I have found that to surface the topic in my own educational management courses is to unveil a plethora of such peak experience and an omnipresent reluctance to talk about them. This reluctance, like my own, can gradually be overcome, with the result that the class gets a firmer sense of exactly wherein lies real satisfaction. I suppose that many, especially from my own organized religious background, will immediately question the "validity" of these experiences. Since I am not a theologian, and since I assume that theological criteria must be brought to bear in such a "challenge," I can only offer the experiences as meeting scientific descriptions of such experiences. And I am not really going to push that argument too far either, since the unique nature of each experience seems to me ultimately to defy any kind of generalization at all. In addition, even if purists would deny the validity of these experiences as reported here, I trust that fact will not undermine their possible interest in the argument that religious education should be aimed at enhancing the probability of such *valid* experiences.

Finally, I guess the only reason that prompted me to proceed in this highly personal way is the hope that such a move on my part might prompt others to do the same. In this way, "naturalistic inquiry" into the considerations of these letters would certainly benefit from an increased amount of information from very diverse sources.

4. Subsequent to the writing of this letter, I did purchase "Holy Family." At the time of my writing this note, we still haven't discussed a cover for the book. We'll see.

5. The poetry I write is very much influenced by my friends, family, students, etc . . . . i.e., what they say, what they do. Thus, *Swansong* I consider to be a joint product of both David and me to a significant extent. On the other hand, to date I have shared the poetry only with my family and friends and this book constitutes a departure for me in this regard. Perhaps the one person I have relied on the most for criticism regarding the transcendental content of the poetry is Fr. Paul A. Byrnes who is the director of the Western Maryland Center for Total Christian Education. Fr. Paul is an old friend of mine from my Saint Charles and Saint Mary's days. With him, I have shared all of the poems which I have written to convey the transcendental experiences I hope to convey. His willingness to react to these poems, given their avowed purpose, in no way should lead one to suggest that he is attesting to their theological validity. His feedback to me has been mainly along lines of helping me to record, in the poetry, my own experiences in the spiritual life with special emphasis on helping me recast the poems so that their presentation does not obfuscate their purpose.

6. John Ashbery, "Litany," in *As We Know* (New York: Viking Penguin, 1979), p. 17.

7. Abraham Maslow, "The 'Core-Religious' or 'Transcendent' Experience," in John White, editor, *The Highest State of Consciousness* (Garden City, N.Y.: Doubleday and Co., Anchor Books, 1972), pp. 352–364.

8. Plato, "The Republic," in W. H. D. Rouse, translator, Eric H. Warmington, and Philip G. Rouse, editors, *Great Dialogues of Plato* (The New American Library, A Mentor Book), pp. 312–341.

9. Swami Probhavananda and Christopher Isherwood, translators, *Bhagavad-Gita,* (New York: The New American Library, 1956), p. 92.

10. This following brief section on ecumenical transcendental

experiences leans almost completely on Geoffrey Parinder's excellent *Mysticism in the World's Religions*. (New York: Oxford University Press, 1976), *passim*. It provides a ready reference rich in examples of peak experiences as they are found ecumenically in the world's organized traditions of religious experience.

11. Chris Argyris, "Individual Actualization in Complex Organizations" in Fred D. Carver and Thomas J. Sergiovanni, editors, *Organizations and Human Behavior: Focus on Schools* (New York: McGraw Hill, 1969), pp. 189–199.

12. Abraham Maslow, *Eupsychian Management* (Homewood, Ill.: Richard D. Irwin, Inc., 1965), pp. 17–33.

Letter III

Dear Jim,

I am a bit confused about this feast. It seems it *is* the Baptism of the Lord but so, too, it seems was January 6th, which heretofore I had always thought was the Feast of the Three Kings, exclusively. Well, at any rate the celebration of the Lord's baptism is today . . . of that I am sure.

Regarding this feast, it has been pointed out that even Christ himself went through the "outward sign" requirements of religion, an allusion no doubt to the fact that I could probably take some inspiration from such a divine attitude in light of my own wary view of bureaucratic (including ecclesiastical) procedures. Still, it seems to me that Christ did indeed perform within the "outward sign" affairs of pre-Christian Judaism but, in this case at least, the organized ritual of John's baptism was, if any thing, *anti*bureaucratic, and a source of consternation to both political and religious bureaucrats of the day.

I said that this letter would be a discussion of religious education, as defined in the previous letter, and the social sciences. What I will try to do is bring to bear concepts and motifs from the social sciences which, I think, have a lot to say as far as deeper understanding of religious education and of its ecumenical nature. But first, in what might look like a digression,

40

I have to tell you a story of the Three Kings and some of the children from the Uptown YMCA. Actually, the story is not totally a digression. It should help us keep our sights focused on where the "action" is in religious education in addition to pointing us ultimately to the next letter which will be an effort to draw practical implications out of our social science deliberations.

RAY MENDEZ AND THE THREE KINGS

As you know, I am chairperson of a small Spanish, black, Haitian, and white YMCA here on the upper west side known as the Uptown YMCA. We are probably the smallest and poorest YMCA in the world . . . currently we are losing $40,000 a year. In an effort to raise some money, we sponsored our first annual celebration of *La Fiesta de los Tres Reyes Magos* on January 6, 1981. However, our basic purpose was to heighten our Spanish communities' awareness and appreciation of their heritage in which this feast figures very prominently and to involve the other communities (i.e., Haitian, black, white, etc.) for similar reasons in light of the intrinsic ecumenical nature of the feast. (As Amahl points out, "One of them is black!")

Last Tuesday (January 6th), our co-director, George Mederos, gave me the high sign, and I found myself in front of the assembled revelers with three Spanish children who were more interest in the coming attack on the piñata than in me. Undaunted, however, I held a small group session, a fishbowl, with the kids, having them tell me what they knew about the story of the Three Kings.

At one point I must have asked where the Baby Jesus came from, because little Ray Mendez proudly announced on the basis of his four-year experience, that the baby Jesus had come "from his mommy's stomach."

Still undaunted, relentlessly in pursuit of my religious education goals, I proceeded to probe the kids about the wondrous and miraculous way in which the Three Kings came from very far away (north and east of Harlem!) and still they found the Baby, and not any old baby but THE RIGHT BABY. How, I asked, could such a remarkable thing have happened?

Now the staff, board members, guests, etc. were ready with little flashlights to simulate the starlight from the heavens as part of an effort to enhance this multimedia religious education presentation. Little did we know they would not be needed. For, as you will see, in the minds of at least one of these children, the starlight was superfluous.

When I asked the question as to the accuracy of the Three Kings in finding their appropriate destination in the presence of the Baby Jesus, one little girl avowed as how an angel had directed them in a dream and a little boy did aver that, indeed, a star had led them. But before I could capitalize on any of these responses, little Ray Mendez quite simply, but quite audibly and quite definitely, asserted that, "THE CAMEL KNEW." This time, I *was* daunted. The childlike response with its simplicity, purity, and unabashed faith was overwhelming. And . . . so much for our flashlights and so much for a recent *New York Times* article alleging the star of Bethlehem was a supernova. Who needs all these gimmicks when faced with a child's God-given insight into this religious situation? The more I think about it, why wouldn't the camel know?

When I told my sister-in-law Carole about this occurrence, she cherished it as I knew she would and indicated that children often see the truths of our mysteries much more clearly than we. Then, too, I was reminded of Ingrid Bergman and Bing Crosby in *The Bells of Saint Mary*. "Sister Ingrid" invites

"Father Bing" to watch a rehearsal of the first-grade Christmas pageant. As it proceeds with humor and insight, Sister Ingrid says, "I never know what they are going to do. They do it differently every time." Let me take this opportunity, too, to vouchsafe the genuineness of Ray's performance. Contrary to a lot of well-meaning but suspicious "Uptowners," Ray and I had not even rehearsed.

Digression over, it's time to bring some social science motifs to bear on religious education as I have described it. The two motifs that I will focus on for present purposes are these of "values" and "transcendental states."

VALUES

Values are beliefs we hold about reality. They are our personal priorities which shape our behavior in its most gross and its most subtle dimensions. Classically, values in social science cluster together to form *ethoi,* or subcultures, and, in turn, these subcultures cluster together to form cultures. Thus, for example, certain values like individualism and delayed gratification cluster with others to form the middle-class ethos or subculture; the middle-class ethos and other subcultures such as the economic and power elite and the lower socioeconomic minority groups make up the American culture. Such at least is my reading of Talcott Parsons, especially as he is translated for educators by his outstanding student, Jack Getzels, from the University of Chicago.[1]

As we look at these values today, however, we have to agree that things are shifting. Spindler has indicated that while we still have traditional values evident in the American culture, a new set of "emergent" values is with us.[2] It is this phenomenon which is of special interest to religious educators.

The emergent values, at least in my study of them, are so evidently emergent that in at least one instance they may be said *to have arrived*. Briefly, the shift from traditional to emergent which is of concern to us here is the shift from the value (traditional) of *delayed gratification* to *immediate gratification* (emergent). Consider if you will the "humor" we find in Archie Bunker's "stifle yourself," as opposed to the "do it now" generation of disco-mania and the drug culture.

This shift in even predominant values in the culture surrounding religious education experiences has deep ramifications. Most (not all) religions consciously or unconsciously promote the traditional value of delayed gratification for the sake of future gain. Whereas heretofore most religions could assume a somewhat supportive value system surrounding their efforts, at least in America and Europe, now, such a support system is, if not absent, at least severely threatened. Indeed, I think the reason that attendance at religious affairs is definitely down rests in the power of this immediate gratification ethic. It is evident even among my graduate students who come traditionally from the most conservative of professions. Yet, as I poll them year after year, the power of this immediate gratification ethic is in evidence even among them.

What response should religious education make to this shift in values? Should it sell out to the immediate gratification trend and forgo its long-range goals? Such a suggestion is certainly a bit silly, but I wish I could say I have never met a clergyman who had so "sold out." Unfortunately, I cannot say that. But there is a response I can suggest, and indeed I have already suggested. The response is to pitch the religious instruction in the direction of enhancing the probability that people, here and now, will achieve a "high," will attain to a transcendental state of mind. In short, religious education designed to foster "peak" experiences is religious education designed to respond to and to make sense to followers of the powerful emergent ethic of "carpe diem," once of poetical and historical interest, but now a very real and living force in every community.

A look at values theory and research from the social sciences, then, reveals a shift in dominant cultural values with which religious education must come to grips. A conclusion for religious education from such value studies points in the direction of a religious education that promises and delivers experiences of high "cosmic consciousness."

TRANSCENDENTAL STATES

The second motif from the social sciences that I bring to bear on religious education is that of "transcendental state" (i.e., peak experience, mysticism, cosmic consciousness).

In a previous letter I have tried to indicate what these experiences look like across the world's religions. Now I would like to take a look at what these experiences look like from a social science perspective. First of all, I have already alluded to the fact that social scientists urged the attainment of these states even in the workplace. What we have to say here, then, will have significant import for whatever practical applications we wish to derive for religious education in the next letter. For the religious education setting is task-oriented, subject to and reflecting the same principles as operate for effectiveness and efficiency in production.

What the social sciences tell us about these peak experiences is that every one of us has a need to have them. This is only to say, in our terms, then, that we all have religious needs. The fun part about the social science approach is, however, inherent in the fact that this need has now been theoretically and empirically established, researched, and isolated so that a clearer understanding of its importance is no longer a matter of faith but a matter of scientific fact.

Maslow

Maslow's hierarchy of needs is a very powerful tool. For all its drawbacks, it remains, especially for people in human resources development, a key framework and tool. Industrial training directors report that Maslow is "number two man" in influence both in theory and practice among human resources trainers and developers. (Number one is Peter Drucker.) Maslow's work has been applied to teachers, and five needs of teachers themselves as working are listed hierarchically. They are:

1. security
2. affiliation
3. self-esteem
4. autonomy
5. self-actualization[3]

Although these are listed above as teachers needs, these same needs in this same hierarchy operate in children and adults with some slight variances.

It is not my purpose here to go into all the ins-and-outs of this theory. Lots of space could be devoted to establishing exactly how stable and consistent the hierarchy of needs is. For our purposes we will simply note that lower needs, in general, have to be met before higher needs are met. But, especially in the case of mystics like Teresa of Avila, John of the Cross, etc. at some point or other the hierarchy goes out the window in favor of a direct move by the Holy Spirit who, like the wind, has a tendency to blow where and when she will.

But, you may ask, what have Saint Teresa of Avila, John of the Cross, etc. to do with Maslow's hierarchy of needs? Well, it seems pretty clear that in what experts call "the later Maslow," his motif of *self-actualization,* the need at the top of the hierarchy, turns out to be none other than the need for transcendence, the need to experience mystic states, the need to revel in the ecstacy of cosmic consciousness.[4]

Now this contribution of the "later Maslow" is important for a lot of reasons. It is important because it has a) ramifications for the relationship between religion and the workplace, b) import for an understanding of human nature such that such a need is seen as common and not "special" or unique, and c) quite heuristic implications within the social sciences themselvess for it constitutes a link between Maslow and the classic work on the organization and administration of the production site, *The Functions of the Executive,* by Chester I. Barnard.[5]

For the mature Maslow to have found the need for transcendence as important to workplace managers is most significant. It, for me anyway, puts a new light on the relationship between work and religion. Heretofore, only the highest levels of sociological theory have linked different economic systems with the various religious postures of mankind. Weber, for example, saw a relationship between the Judaeo-Christian ethic and capitalism while the economic posture of India was seen as directly related to the omnipresence of Brahman (Atman) in Hinduism. I don't think I have to go into this here. It seems sufficient to note that religion and economics have been linked before.

What Maslow seems to be saying, however, is somewhat different. He is saying that the workplace should be designed to meet the same need as religion, at least as we have viewed religion in these letters. If this is so, a new kind of direct link between religion and the workplace seems to have come to light. If the workplace is not designed ultimately to meet this mystic need, then, in addition to lowered productivity, one can anticipate an even greater burden on religion to foster the meeting of this need. In addition, one can envision a very heavy mutual effort to "up" mutual productivity.

I hasten to point out that what we are discussing is the "discovery" of a *theoretical* link between religion and the workplace. Experience over the centuries indicates a very obvious relationship between work and religion ranging from Benedict's "To work is to pray" to the day-to-day observed productivity of religious workers who are known to their managers to be more productive than their nonreligious confreres. While this latter instance may be too often a function of forces not all that transcendence oriented, the theoretical finding seems to be that the transcendence force emitted by meeting the self-actualization need is legitimately construed as causative of increased productivity. While abuses of coercion (e.g., from within a sect) and exploitation (e.g., from within managerial circles) abound, beyond this exploitation and coercion rests the fact of the force of the need for transcendence, once met, to increase productivity.

I'll further address this close relationship between religion and work in the next letter. It has, as I hope to point out, great practical implications, not the least of which is career-oriented religious education.

Still another important aspect of the later contributions of Maslow is the notion of the universality of the need for transcendence. I have alluded to this point before but, I think it important to emphasize it again. We, all of us, have this need for mystical experience. None of us is deficient in this category. Therefore, all of us deserve to be put in situations where we have the chance of meeting this ultimate need. To do otherwise to us is to put us in spirit-killing environments with disastrous consequences not only for ourselves but for the culture in which we live. It is not, as Plato would have it, that some of us are doomed to be hewers of wood and drawers of water without the chance of transcending. Nor are some of us the privileged few who transcend and govern. Quite the contrary, all of us are to transcend and all occupations are quite comfortable with the transcending individual.

Now, this notion of the universality of the need to transcend does not usually sit too well with the tough-nosed realists I deal with in my public education seminars. And even if my students can be brought to see the theoretical viability of such a universal need, they rarely see immediately the down-to-earth implications of such a need. Indeed, I find that most of them are either unaware of their own need to transcend or . . . and perhaps this is more important . . . even though they are aware of their need to transcend they are reluctant to make the transcendental experience public. Once their lack of awareness is overcome, however, and once their initial reluctance to share such experiences is vanquished, not only does the theoretical viability of this Maslovian insight shine forth but its practical day-to-day impact is also felt, replete with its universality.

The third important aspect of this later Maslow contribution is the bridge it constitutes between Maslow (and third-force psychology in general) and the social science classic on organizations and their management, Chester Barnard's *The Functions of the Executive*. The nature of this link is what I would like to establish now. Since we are construing the religious education setting as an instance of the organized workplace, such a link gives us an even stronger reason to explore such a classic treatise in light of our transcendence goal for religious education. If Barnard's study can be seen as predating Maslow's "mystical" workplace hypothesis, then these two giants of social science history can be seen as harbingers of great import for those of us who would "up" the productivity of the religious education workplace.

To proceed; while I have heretofore almost identified the theory with Maslow, we find after investigation that the same theory is prevalent in Chester Barnard's *The Functions of the Executive,* the original social science treatise on organizations, the last line of which is "out of the void comes the spirit to shape the ends of men."[6]

Barnard

Now, when I start talking this way in my university classes with people in public education, they at first suspect me of being a little bit spooky. Gradually, however, by weaving Maslow and Barnard, we begin to get a look at any organized activity such that the ultimate need to be addressed in the organized setting (in any organized setting including religious education) is the need to transcend the here and now, to trip out, to experience a "high," to peak, to experience cosmic conscious, to experience that "organization of organizations in which all men live boundlessly."[7]

Let me turn directly now to the Barnard classic, for it is in its pages that I feel I have found an alternative way of conceiving and delivering any service . . . alternative that is, to what we see around us. For, and this seems not to be just my perception, education in general and religious education in particular appear to be in some sort of holding pattern, or decline. I was very upset when a local religious elementary school was closed. And yet, surrounded by streets of immediate gratification made even more alluring by being seen from a condition of poverty, it seems the drawing power of the school was nil. And when on Sunday morning I watch the small numbers of Sunday School students head for the regular Sunday session, I wonder what this means for the future. In addition, I feel it is not sufficient simply to say that the ethic of immediate gratification has done our religious organizations in. I fear they, themselves, have aided and abetted the process through the unconscious adoption of bureaucratic principles which are essentially destined to kill the Christ in all of us unless they are radically adjusted out of the traditional Weberian mode.

The alternative which Chester Barnard posits in his book is at first a little surprising if not downright offensive, especially to my bureaucratic friends. For, if I may paraphrase him in his Appendix: "When the computer says to go to the right, when the vice presidents tell you to go to the right, and your wife tells you to go to the right, and you still feel you should go to the left . . . . *go to the left.*" In other words, when all the logic tells you one thing and you still feel the opposite, do the opposite . . . i.e., be nonlogical.[8]

As I ask my students from the public schools, when was the last time someone urged you to be nonlogical? Barnard, however, gets even "more curiouser." Throughout the book you see him struggling with being logical and nonlogical, and you are left somewhat confused for quite a while as to what he means by *nonlogical.* Early on, however, it becomes clear to the reader that whatever Barnard means by being nonlogical, he does not mean being whimsical or capricious. This is not the book of a whimsical and capricious man. Whatever he means by nonlogical is something beyond logic, something which is actually positive, and something which actually "controls" logic itself. What is it?

Clair Myers Owens in the late sixties reminded us that "years ago Bertrand Russell wrote that the person who has had mystical experience is above logic. He has been there; he knows."[9] Is it possible that there is a mystical experience hovering at the center of Barnard's theory of all organized life?

Before we answer that question, a look at Barnard's pedigree might at least encourage the reader at this point to pay him careful attention. Can a book that ends with "out of the void comes the spirit" even be considered a social science book? *And,* even if it is, what indeed does it have to do with religious education? I will try to demonstrate that it can explain, together with the emergent values phenomenon we have discussed above, the holding pattern and/or decline of religious education. It can also put us in a growth-oriented mode.

As you might well imagine, Barnard's pedigree is impeccable. Indeed, it was awareness of this pedigree which made me seriously question early the commonplace interpretation given to Barnard's *Functions.* I can still remember the first read-out I got on him in one of my classes at Notre Dame. What I was receiving was what turned out to be just about everybody else's interpretation of the work. But as the professor—not you, of course, but a less-valued colleague—in all good conscience proceeded to describe Barnard as fostering behavioral and systematic (only!) approaches to organizational well-being, I think you will remember I began to squirm. That was not, if I was reading the text correctly, what Barnard was all about. When, thanks directly to you in many ways, I arrived at the University of Chicago and met Jack Getzels, then the enigma of Barnard began to clear up. (Remember when you drove me to Chicago for that initial interview there?)

For Jack is a most worthy protege of the late Talcott Parsons, who was perhaps America's greatest sociologist. It was with Jack's encouragement and support that I completed a detailed comparison between Barnard and Parsons. Barnard, at his central theoretical definition of organization, cites Parsons: "The concept of the group as the dominant characteristic of cooperative systems is certainly also frequent in the literature of sociology, anthropology, and social psychology, although as shown by Parsons, systems in which at least the emphasis is upon action have been fundamental in the conceptual schemes of Durkheim, Pareto, and Weber."[10] Barnard's own footnote refers to Parsons's *The Structure of Social Action*,[11] a book which I had to read thirteen times (slow-learner but over-achiever that I am) before I could even talk reasonably about it.

The question then arose as to the extent of Parsons's influence on Barnard. This extent is what I documented in my own dissertation and need not concern us in detail here. What appears to be the case is that Barnard's *Functions* is Parsons's *Structure* "writ small" and focused as it were on organizational life. Certainly this was no mean feat. For in effect, then, in *The Functions* we have a distillation of Parsons's own analysis of and conclusions from Marshall, Pareto, Durkheim, and Weber. As I tell my students, mastery of Barnard gives them more than a leg up on the mastery of significant research in the social sciences for the last two-hundred years.

Barnard is, then, not only of high pedigree by dint of his Parsonian influence, he is also the social scientist (theoretical) par excellence, proffering the weary executive/manager, in capsule form, the wisdom of the social science sages who have preceded him.

And what does Barnard say to this beleaguered organizational type? He says that executives and managers who are successful know something that other people don't. He says that there is an "executive state of mind," the "executive intuition." The contents of this executive intuition are what Barnard spells out in this text. How does he do it? By applying the findings of the great social scientists. And what exactly are the "contents" of the executive intuition?

That's what I hope to pinpoint for you. I am going to zero in on the nature of the executive intuition which Barnard says is necessary to the effective and efficient running of any human organization. I will try to demonstrate that the executive intuition is *mystically based,* and is a Maslow "peak experience." But before I do, by way of introduction (if not apologia) for what I am about to do, here's a poem I wrote which seems to have something to say to where we've been in these letters and where we're going. I hope it helps.

PINPOINT: A HARD THING TO DO

Apophatically speaking it's not the head which
leaves   out
angels, perhaps
nevertheless, it has upon a Cajun
required a cushion
this cushioned occasion for indianhead pennies
can hardly be the other end of a pin, can it?

a sharp question this requiring a sharp reply
which can only be a question
why did the angels dance on the other hand
why couldn't they just *be* on the other end?
Are they all that happy?
Certainly if they did whatever it is they do on the point of a
    pin
it probably would be better to dance . . . on point, of
    course
and counter point and so the theologians do go on
obfuscating in a logosphere the simple river of truth
which because it won't be pinned down, and here is the
point.

And here are some further points............
but u see ur all the same point so lets do the
pinhead or pinpoint polka with the polski pope
the roman rabbi the african buddha..........

And I must go now . . . Suzuki awaits . . . and flowers and
   butterflies
surround me as I dance . . . o please
and when I looked at one under a magnifying glass
I expected to see perhaps a self-portrait in an unbreakable
magnifying lens but instead I saw
Cleopatra's needle which is a bit like this
poem inasmuch as I feel I am searching for a needle in a
haystack but its only to pinpoint I seek
and I wish you would let me be obscure because that is the
point

beneath the shit of everyday commerce is the simplicity of
oneness which is itself not obscure but we sure have
secured it up
and why should I continue to add to this clutter of eons
in the beginning was the word and one word was
obviously enough but then again maybe it really
allisonewordwewriteanditisalwaysthesamewordthroughall
eternitywearethewordofgodnewworldwithoutendamen

I wrote this poem on a dare from a young English poet,
Kenneth Fuchs. He was interested in the way I wrote and
suggested I try writing on something insignificant and commonplace. What you have just read is the result. And, for
present purposes, looking for a mystical basis in Barnard's
executive intuition is not only highly out of the ordinary (both
colleagues and students over the years will attest to this) but
sometimes it is like looking for a needle in a haystack or, in
other words, difficult to pinpoint.

Nevertheless, taking a cue from Bertrand Russell, we are
drawn to Barnard's definition of *logical* as something that can
be *articulated*.[12] And, pursuing his argument further, something that can be articulated is *not* sufficient to organizational

success. Rather, we have to achieve the *non*logical. This could easily be Russell's "beyond logic" and indeed the top executive behavior which Barnard describes is, in Russell's terms, the behavior of a man who has seen and been there and is no longer purely a function of reasoning.

In the poem above, I suggest in a Platonic sense that there is a oneness which we all can and must grasp underneath the fuss and bother of our day-to-day existence. And constantly throughout his text Barnard seems to be arguing for decision making always in the context of what he terms the sense of the "whole."[13] But what is the whole?

Briefly, the *whole* which the successful manager "grasps" intuitively is the *organization* itself which Barnard describes as a living being unto itself, greater than the sum of its parts, not made up of the individuals who are affiliated with it, not even existing primarily in space, and not to even be conceived of as a group. What is the living being which, in Barnard's thought, seems to have a mind and will of its own over and above the minds and wills of its "members"?[14] Whatever it is, it is something real, union with which is union with something greater than oneself. It would appear to be an entity midway between the individual and the cosmos. As such it is noteworthy. But what about "the beyond" . . . i.e. what about mystic cosmic consciousness?

What I am *not* going to do in the next page or two of this letter is establish a *close* congruence between Barnard and Maslow. I do not think that such a congruence can be effected, although I could be wrong. I doubt very much if anyone as heavily influenced by Parsons would find a close, point by point agreement with one of the foremost thinkers of "third-force psychology." I hasten to point out, however, that I am not necessarily convinced that there may not eventually turn out to be a close alignment of Barnard's and Maslow's thought. Indeed, for all his Parsonian roots, Jack Getzels has never hesitated to link Maslow's hierarchy of needs with his Parsons-rooted social systems model, something we will be looking at more closely in the next letter. For our purpose, however, all we are looking for is a similiarity of one motif, i.e., the transcendent, enhanced state of consciousness.

Let us begin looking for a Maslow-like cosmic consciousness in Barnard by returning to his definition of *logical*. Barnard says in this Appendix: "By 'logical processes' I mean conscious thinking which could be expressed in words, or other symbols. . . . By 'nonlogical' processes I mean those not capable of being expressed in words or as reasoning."[15] So, this nonlogical element in Barnard is "ineffable," the word Maslow used to describe peak experience. But surely this is just a semantic likeness into which we cannot read too much. Possibly, but consider this. In his Preface Barnard practically admits to a severe weakness in his text. For a man who has set out to spell out the contents of the executive intuition, to confess in his Preface that he has insufficiently, in the text, spelled out the "executive mental processes," is not only to overwhelm the reader with his humility, but to put the reader on guard . . . seriously on guard . . . as to the exact meaning of what he is about to read. In his Preface Barnard says:

> Still more do I regret the failure to convey the sense of organization, the dramatic and aesthetic feeling that surpasses the possibilities of exposition, which derives chiefly from the intimate habitual interested experience. It is evident that many lack interest in the science of organization because they are oblivious to the arts of organizing, not perceiving the significant elements. They miss the structure

of the symphony, the art of its composition, and the skill of its execution, because they cannot hear the tones.

Copies of my Cyrus Fogg Brackett Lecture given at Princeton University on March 10, 1936 were distributed to the audience at the Lowell Institute primarily as an aid to understanding the present chapters XIII and XIV. It is reprinted here as an Appendix for the same purpose, and because in general it explains some aspects of the behavior of executives, especially their mental processes, not sufficiently treated in the main text.[16]

"Wow!" says I. These are not the words of a behaviorist! And this fact becomes even more clear when we examine the Appendix itself. This aspect of the executive psyche, so inarticulable . . . so ineffable . . . (that it even escaped being explicated in the main text!) . . . is described in the Appendix as appropriate to the major executive, the contents of whose mind is described as follows: "Logical processes (are) increasingly necessary but are disadvantageous if not in subordination to highly developed intuitional processes."[17] Now, when was the last time you heard of logic as being "disadvantageous"? But now that we see the crucial importance of these nonlogical processes, we still are left somewhat confused as to their exact nature? And, much to behaviorist consternation and bureaucratic frustration, these processes are described as a matter of "sensing," of "feeling," the result of experience which is superior to reasoning although reasoning is a good way to check out the accuracy of the initial "hunches" and intuition. To Barnard, reason is the "handmaiden" of intuition, much as some people would say philosophy is a handmaiden to theology.

If you are with me so far, you are probably still wondering what all this has to do with Maslow. That Maslow's peak experience is an ineffable intuition seems clear. But clearly not all ineffable intuitions are peak experiences. Can it be established that Barnard is talking about anything beyond and above the nonlogical intuition that one attributes to a salesman, a teacher, etc. . . . or any woman for that matter?

Well, he seems to be. But, as he himself said, he was not satisfied with his textual presentation of this executive intuition. As evidence, however, that he is ascribing a "religious" peak experience to the executives, the following passage seems appropriate: "Executive responsibility, then, is that capacity of leaders by which, reflecting attitudes, ideals, hopes, derived largely from without themselves, they are compelled to bind the wills of men to the accomplishment of purposes beyond their immediate ends, beyond their times. Even when these purposes are lowly and the time is short, the transitory efforts of men become a part of that organization of living forces that transcends man unaided by man; but when these purposes are high and the wills of many men in many generations are bound together they live boundlessly. . . . So among those who cooperate the things that are seen are moved by the things unseen. Out of the void comes the spirit that shapes the ends of men."[18]

And, at the very conclusion of the text, having indicated that all through the text he has been struggling with the exact balance which should exist between the individual and the organization, he says: "Because it is subjective with respect to society as a whole and to the individual, what this proportion is I believe science cannot say. It is a question for philosophy and religion."[19]

What are we to make of all this? Barnard himself admits to struggling to get this across. What I maintain is that Barnard is talking about, at least at the top executive positions, the same experience that Maslow talks about. And curiously, Maslow brought this thinking to management, also. To quote *him* again: "We must ultimately assume at the highest theoretical levels of Eupsychian theory, a preference or tendency to identify with more and more of the world, moving toward the ultimate of mysticism, a fusion with the world, or peak experience, cosmic consciousness."[20]

Jim, do you agree? Do you see Barnard as proffering "cosmic consciousness" as being at the highest theoretical levels in his thought (as well as the highest executive levels)? And do you see Maslow as saying much the same thing? I am not arguing here for total congruence between these two great minds. But I do see a remarkable similarity and, ultimately, a complementarity. Both social scientists are talking religion, when push comes to shove. Both are proffering arguments that seriously impugn hyperrationalization of action in organized settings.

If you do agree, then you see that the father of organizational science, Chester Barnard, and one of our leading human development proponents, Abraham Maslow, have investigated the workplace and found therein the essential "play" of the mystical experience. Granted that this is so, the religious education experience, viewed as the workplace (with teachers as workers and students as partially socialized workers) can make a response to the "immediate gratification" ethic of the day. Certainly the response is not to abandon long-range personal development with sacrifice and delayed gratification. But the response can relate to much of the flavor of the "do it now," and "do your own thing" generation, and even to the substance. For the "do it now," "do your own thing" modern "carpe diem" generation is fascinated by the pursuit of the "ultimate high." Granted many of them seem to lock themselves in at levels of experience where the drug-, alcohol-, sex-induced high is probably more ersatz then genuine. But many of them are continually striving for that "high" without benefit of chemical, physical stimulus. The growth of the westernized Eastern religions is a case in point and their success is due, in my estimation, to their partial but significant appeal to the "emergent" value of today's population. They promise a "high."

Can religious education take this posture in general? I think so. In so doing, it will ensconce itself well within age-old religious traditions of ecstatic experience religiously derived. It will also ensconce itself in a position where it can benefit from the more systematic insights of the social sciences. In short, any organized activity, and especially the workplace, is rife with potential mystical experience. Why not the religious education workplace?

Unfortunately, we do have to admit that most of our workplaces appear to us to be the last place where such transcendental experiences are available. All too true. But does not our economic and productivity record currently indicate that something is amiss? Are not the obvious failures of our public schools matched by similar failures in our religious education settings? The question is obviously a rhetorical one.

Something is wrong; something is destroying the effectiveness and efficiency of our institutions, something that has not failed to downgrade the effects of even our religious institutions. What that something is is the hyperrationality of the classic Weberian bureacratic model which, in its ruthless application to all areas of human endeavor, has managed to all but preclude the occurrence of peak, intuitive, mystical, ecstatic experience in any workplace, including the religious education workplace. I think it safe to say that bureaucrats and most modern corporate types are "nonpeakers." Indeed, the hyperorganization's dysfunctional tendency to prohibit the circulation of the talented elite, to reward mediocrity, to abort creative excellence, etc. all point to the same effect. The creative peak experience is no longer at home in our institutions, religious or otherwise. And I hasten to point out that it is exactly this kind of peak experience which would significantly accommodate any institution to the surrounding environment of immediate gratification. For, both religiously and scientifically, this experience is not only a "high" attainable by all, it is better than any "high" attainable on most streets, or in dormitories, pornshops, and saloons. One might even call it "seductive."

I'll close this one for now in the hope that I have used values theory and motifs on transcendence from the social sciences to pose and explicate the problem of religious education today and to offer a potential solution. The "how" of all this is my next responsibility. So in the next letter I will deal with practical implications for religious educators of the hypotheses presented in this letter.

MAY today's "highs" be tomorrow's "lows."
DAVID

Notes to Letter III

1. Jacob W. Getzels, James M. Lipham, and Roald F. Campbell, *Educational Administration as a Social Process: Theory, Research, Practice* (New York: Harper & Row, 1968).

2. The following discussion of values leans heavily on G. O. Spindler's work as it is reported and incorporated into the Getzels's work on social systems theory in Getzels et al., *Educational Administration as a Social Process,* pp.96–102.

3. This lineup of the hierarchy of needs is actually a variation of Maslow's presentation developed by Lyman Porter and reported in Thomas J. Sergiovanni and Fred D. Carver *The New School Execu-*

tive: A Theory of Administration, 2nd edition (New York: Harper & Row, 1980), p. 84. The variation on the original Maslow is presented as more appropriate to teachers' needs.

4. Abraham Maslow, "The 'Core-Religious,' or 'Transcendental Experience' " in Jonn White, editor, *The Highest State of Consciousness* (Garden City, N.Y.: Doubleday and Co., 1972), pp. 352–364.

5. Chester I. Barnard, *The Functions of the Executive* (Cambridge, Mass.: Harvard University Press, 1964). Barnard's original text is copyrighted in 1938. It is a sort of bible in the management field. The interpretation of the work which follows is uncommon, probably because the Second World War reduced its immediate significance. The onslaught of behaviorism subsequent to the war saw the work fitting the behavioral perception of the world. That it does not can be established on a point for point basis, even in light of Barnard's espousal of the work of Herbert Simon in the latter's early years. Later Simon can be seen as reflecting Barnard's original treatise. That is to say that later Simon reflects the influence of the nonlogical. intuitive side of management more than his earlier work. There is common recognition of the later Simon contributions, witness his recent Nobel Prize in economics.

6. Ibid., p. 284.

7. Ibid.

8. Ibid., p. 322.

9. Clair Myer Owens, "The Mystical Experience: Facts and Values" in John White, editor, *The Highest State of Consciousness,* (Garden City, N.Y.: Doubleday, Anchor Books, 1972), p. 137.

10. Barnard, *The Functions of the Executive,* pp. 68–69.

11. Talcott Parsons, *The Structure of Social Action* (New York: McGraw-Hill, 1937).

12. Barnard, *The Functions of the Executive,* p. 302.

13. Ibid., pp. 238–239; 322.

14. Ibid., pp. 79–80, 259. At this point it seems worthwhile to point out that this kind of "intermediary being" which is the "living system of human efforts" that is the organization is quite necessary to the practicality of Barnard's theory . . . as impractical (and improbable) as it may first appear to my colleagues in the management

sciences. For this actual living "praeter-human" entity affords Barnard a view of human responsibility which has most practical, day-to-day implications. But, perhaps more interestingly, this praeter-human being affords Barnard the most powerful of human motivators. These, however, are matters for a more management-oriented book than this. The point is that, as "transcendent" as the Barnard hypothesis appears to be, its pragmatic implications are huge.

15. Barnard, *The Functions of the Executive,* p. 302.

16. Ibid., p. xiv.

17. Ibid., p. 320.

18. Ibid., p. 283–284.

19. Ibid., p. 296.

20. Abraham Maslow, *Eupsychian Management* (Homewood, Ill.: Richard D. Irwin, 1965), pp. 17–33.

Letter IV

MARCH 6, 1981

Dear Jim,

Here's a poem to start things off in this letter to you on the "how" of religious education as viewed through social science.

A NEED FOR REDEMPTION

I think that each one of us is
made up differently
True, some of the elements look
alike
but
the relationship between and among
are all ways different always
so that of these complexities of complexities
we call us
some fly apart too easily
some never fly apart
some are apart
although together
and some never fly
If this be so then all truth is fiction
and all fiction is truth and we
drift in the swirling eddies
of South Bend leaf piles

> looking as if we sought general patterns
> to make sense of each gust of wind
> but left unaided we are dead leaves
> That must be what redemption means

I guess I am inserting this poem at this point because we are about to explore practical ways to go about religious education. And as we are viewing it for present purposes, we are going to explore ways, derived from social science research, by which we can enhance the possibility that religious education will enhance and increase the probability that the religious learner will attain to a peak experience now, in the foreseeable future, and in the next life. But the fact of the matter is, as you well know, that whether or not the learner achieves to a transcendental experience is really and ultimately up to God. "Left unaided we are dead leaves. That must be what redemption means." In other words, for all our science and strategies, the final say-so as to our redemption is not up to us. It is up to God.

Does this mean, then, that a quiescent posture is called for—a posture which would have us removed from seeking to consciously enhance the probability of altered states of consciousness? No, that's not what that means at all. Rather, it means that in religious education we have to see ourselves working within the context of God's own redeeming grace, constantly aware of the fact that God can work through us. Indeed, God can even work through the social sciences. They can be, if God permits, a tool of his redemption.

Given this general environment in which to proceed, then, the religious educator can profit greatly, as can the learner, from many contributions of social science to the educative process. I would like to suggest the following ways:

1. The use of social science analytical models
2. Providing prerequisites to transcendental experiences

3. Shaping objectives
4. Career-oriented experiential learning

From a naturalistic inquiry point of perspective, the circumstances in which I write are worth noting.

It's Lent. Sorry for the gap between letters. I have not been idle. The Uptown Y is thriving and we have a real chance of getting access to a pool, gym, etc. The facilities need a lot of work but it's great just to have the chance. My teaching schedule at Pace is horrendous. It is my own doing. Incidentally, the other night when I had a session on Maslow and Barnard and mysticism over at the New York City Board of Education, one student said it was like having a mystical experience and another said it was bullshit.

Finally, this series of letters is, to me anyway, coming along rather well. The only thing that could cause me to miss my book deadline with you is a junket to Egypt which is in the offing for April. Seems the proposal I wrote for an Occupational Training Center at the University of Zagazig is going to be funded, and I have to get a team together and get over there to kick things off. Exciting . . . yes, but I fear for the keeping of this writing schedule, especially because I seem to be on a "roll." I have recently found resources that I am sure will help me to make a contribution in the promised chapters on art and science. And those future chapters will link in to this one through the whole notion of experiential learning.

ANALYTICAL FRAMEWORKS

Back now to the topic at hand, I would first like to address myself to the use of social science analytical frameworks in religious education settings. I know your fondness for using the social sciences for the shaping of objectives along behavioral performance lines. I'll get to this a bit later, but now I am suggesting using social science analytical frameworks to enhance the understanding of religious texts and other phenomena . . . all of this with the ultimate objective in mind of giving the learner a leg up on having a peak experience. Here's an example of what I mean. It has to do with the Getzels's model of a social system and *The Acts of the Apostles*.

A student of mine in the seminars over at the New York City Board of Education, Dermit Kehoe, by name, let it be known that he was, as far as his value complex was concerned, a convert to Anglicanism from Roman Catholicism. It was when he saw the utility of the model presented below to an understanding of himself that he developed the idea of using the model to analyze *The Acts of the Apostles*. The Getzels model[1] (simplified) looks like this:

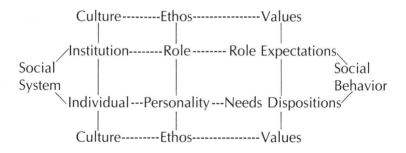

FIGURE 1.   THE GETZELS SOCIAL SYSTEM MODEL

Exactly what this model is and what it enables us to do is interesting but to explain it in detail would be beyond the confines of our purpose. It has been done well in other places and the interested reader will have no difficulty finding a detailed explanation. For our purposes it is enough to say that the model gives us the wherewithal to ask questions objectively and systematically about organized behavior, especially in education. In other words, the model provides a measure of scientific objectivity and an analytical tool enabling us to gather information and ask questions systematically.

Before we proceed, you will note the prevalence of *values* in the framework. It is also of note that Jack Getzels utilizes the Spindler *traditional* and *emergent* categorizations noted in the previous letter. He also is comfortable with using Maslow to further delineate the *needs disposition* element in the model. Therefore, by introducing the model at this point we are on somewhat familiar ground.

In general, what the model tells us is that any organized behavior is a function of the individual and the institutional dimensions. Both the individual and the institution, however, are heavily influenced by values. As one analyzes both individual and institutional dimensions of organized behavior, the impact of values on personalities, needs disposition, roles and role expectations becomes clearer and an explanation for observed behavior as well as alternatives for future behavior become apparent. Here's a quote from Dermit's term project (he applied the model to *The Acts of the Apostles*) which makes my present point better than I can.

This paper has demonstrated to its author, with no small measure of amazement, the applicability of the Getzels-Guba model not only to this book of the New Testament but to other readings and events of religious significance. The model serves as a vehicle for the objective analysis of religious material which would otherwise be highly subjective.

This paper has proceeded in a direction that was far from the intention of the author and has demonstrated the usefulness of the model in objectively analyzing people, actions, and events.[2]

Just as I did not pay Ray Mendez for the "camel" quote noted in the last letter, I did not pay Dermit for this one. The point seems objectively clear. This framework from the social science (and other frameworks) can be exceptionally heuristic to individuals who want to understand themselves and their religious experience better.

Now, practically speaking, what does this mean? It seems to me that, first of all, on the adult level, either as a matter of instruction or as a matter of teacher training, the application of social science models of organized behavior ought to be seriously pursued. Second, while I am not sure that a child like Ray would immediately benefit from such an approach, I am beginning to get evidence, thanks to another student, Doris Peters, that the Getzels model can be consciously used to good effect with intermediate school students. Taking it down any lower in the grades does not bother me, however, since we can also rely on Bruner's theory to the effect that anyone can learn anything at any time in an intellectually honest fashion. Thus, such frameworks might well constitute important input for curriculum in religious education at many levels.

Ultimately, the use of these frameworks can increase understanding of self and religious phenomenon and, therefore, their use can enhance the possibility that the religious learner will experience transcendence. For, in Dermit's quote, it is clear this experience has drawn him even more into his own religious experience, has brought him to the self-esteem-enhancing realization of his own power of objective analysis and has therefore moved him up the Maslow hierarchy of needs to a point where his ability to affiliate and transcend are thereby made more probable. In a sense it could be argued that Dermit's statement already indicates that thanks to his position on

the hierarchy of needs (thanks to the model) he has significantly experienced "coming out of himself" at least to the
point of scientific objectivity in a very personalistic adventure.
Such "scientific transcendence of self" is not a bad start if
one's goal is mystical self-transcendence. It seems to me a
nicely carved-out step along the way. At any rate we can move
now to the next topic in this letter: the providing of prerequisites to the experience of transcendence.

Prerequisites to Transcendence

In their text, *The New School Executive,* Sergiovanni and
Carver present a summary of Maslow's Eupsychian management. They observe at the point where the importance of the
mystical experience for organization surfaces that this assumption of the importance of mysticism is "a challenge to student
alienation, to teacher-administration polarization, and to local
school provincialism."[3] In other words, aiming at mystical
experiences in educational administration, is a powerful rais-
on d'être for meeting "lower level" student needs and "turning them on" instead of off, an indictment of hyperconflicted,
unsatisfying relationships between teachers and administrators, and a goad to the smallest of learning organizations to
expand horizons beyond the local here and now.

As far as student (or teacher) alienation goes, Maslow and
Sergiovanni and Carver are bringing us right back to the
Hawthorne studies, where increased productivity results from
meeting workers needs. From another perspective, we are
faced again with Barnard's definition of efficiency as individual *satisfaction* without which members do not make organizational contributions.[4] But satisfaction of what . . . and
how accomplish this satisfaction?

Referring back to Maslow's hierarchy,[5] what Maslow says is that before you can get anything going at the higher levels of human growth you have to meet the lower physical and biological needs of the individuals involved. Practically speaking then, for religious educators, that means that both teachers and students have to have the *commoda vitae,* the *sine qua non* of interaction. It has been said, in spite of Ronald Reagan's recent impingement thereupon, that one of the most valuable pieces of educational legislation is that which provides breakfast, snacks, and lunch for the learners who otherwise would not have enough food.

It seems to me that the religious educator has to meet this first hierarchical level of needs also. Both teachers and students have to be in a safe, secure, comfortable environment. Teachers have to be supported with sufficient salary, benefits, professional support like tenure, etc. before any additional needs can be met. In religious education it is quite true that these needs are often not necessarily met *directly* by the "authorities" in charge. But these authorities can see that, unless in one way or another these needs are met for teachers, a program leading to peak experiences is highly problematical. From the point of view of the children, much the same, *mutatis mutandis,* seems true. To transcend, you have to eat.

On the next step up the hierarchy of needs, building to transcendence, the social needs seem prevalent. Here again, children as well as teachers need to feel accepted, to experience friendship, and to feel belongingness. The teachers' needs have a good chance, socially speaking, of being met *outside* the religious education setting, in a fashion similar to the way their security needs are often met. This fact, by the way, argues for a questioning of the so-called human relations approach to education (especially in administration) which has been ballyhooed these many years. It also seems clear that another reason for the desirable demise of this human relations approach rests in the observable fact that most "authorities" who claim to espouse this approach are, in reality, nought but shallow, dishonest Machiavellian manipulators.[6]

From the student perspective, however, especially in the child-through-teen years, this social need is very real and the religious education place is a place rich in potential for meeting this need. One way to do it is with a great deal of group work which is, as we will see later on, experienced based.

Now, the next step up on Maslow's stairway to the stars (sic!) is the satisfaction of the need for esteem. This is a need for recognition, self-respect, and, indeed, self-love. To satisfy this need both adult and child have to know and experience accomplishment and to sense that confidence which comes from the self-knowledge of personal competence. I think that your own predeliction for behavioral objectives in religious education has much to say to meeting this need both on the part of teachers and students. For the ubiquitous criterion of effectiveness which haunts all of education is *really* in evidence in religious education where spiritual and long-range goals make for extreme difficulty in assaying one's own success. Wherever possible, explicitly stated behavioral objectives and the wherewithal to evaluate their accomplishment can aid and abet the satisfaction of this need on the part of both teacher and student.

It seems to me that viewing behavioral objectives this way removes from them the patina of mechanistic manipulation from which many good and great teachers naturally shy away. Viewing them in this way puts their use "along the way" (i.e., on a point along the hierarchy of prerequisites) to the development of spiritual perfection. In a sense, then, behavioral objectives facilitate the self-esteem prerequisite to peak experiences. Treated as such they can find their comfortable home within the state of the art of religious education.

Thus, bringing teachers and students to self-esteem through such techniques as behavioral objectives, we can then, still using Lyman Porter's version of Maslow (rendered more precise for education), move the focus of our educational activities to meeting teachers' and students' needs for autonomy. Everyone needs to feel "in control" of his or her own environment and fate; to feel self-responsible; to feel and be free in the "Dewey" sense of freedom. This autonomy need, once met, is like a finding of oneself. But it is not selfishness. For, as we will see, at this stage in the hierarchy we are finding the self so that we can lose the self, thereby meeting the need for self-actualization.

At this point we have begun to build a strategy for religious education which is aimed at bringing us to the increased probability of fostering transcendental experiences by meeting prerequisite needs, such as the biological needs and the need for autonomy.

At this juncture I think we have to face a rather sensitive but practical issue. *Who is qualified to teach?* What I am suggesting in this book is that the end of religious education is the transcendental peak experience, i.e., the meeting of the highest-level need. Can then individuals who have not achieved these peak experiences function in religious education, especially as teachers? Can those whose highest-level needs have not been met, teach others to meet their own highest-level needs? How practical is it to assume that nonpeakers can produce peakers?

It is important to point out at this time that, unlike Plato, there is no cutoff point on the way to transcendence. Thus, it is not true that after a certain point some of us are consigned to being "drawers of water and hewers of wood" and others of us are privileged exclusively to attain to "the light." Rather, the work of Bruner, Bloom, and Maslow points in the direction of everybody being capable of everything, with very few exceptions. Since, then, everyone is capable of the mystic state, my basic impulse is to say that only those who have achieved it should teach in order to enhance the probability that others will do the same. And there is little doubt that an increasing number of people are reaching for and achieving these heights of direct experience of God. Unfortunately, this type of person does not seem to inhabit the upper echelons of our large corporations and massive bureaucracies. In light of this rather depressing fact, I would imagine that these nonpeaking types will undoubtedly reject or severely qualify the approach to religious education taken in the letters. Worse yet, they might yield it lip-service.

Nevertheless, the type of religious education I am advocating can only be delivered by those who have been "there"— those who have, in Teilhard de Chardin's term, "seen." Anything else, it seems to me, would have to be fraud (and there's a lot of that around) or misguided effort (a good deal of which is certainly in evidence). Who said that the road to hell was paved with good intentions?

In saying this, I am not saying anything all that new. In his Introduction to the Bhagavad-Gita, Aldous Huxley says: "The second doctrine of the Perennial Philosophy—that it is possible to know the Divine Ground by a direct intuition higher than discursive reasoning—is to be found in all the great religions of the world. A philosopher who is content merely to know about the ultimate reality—theoretically and by hearsay—is compared by Buddha to a herdsman of other men's cows. Mohammed uses an even homelier barnyard metaphor. For him the philosopher who has not realized his metaphysics is just an ass bearing a load of books. Christian, Hindu, and

Taoist teachers wrote no less emphatically about the absurd pretensions of mere learning and analytical reasoning. In the words of the Anglican Book of Prayer, our eternal life, now and hereafter, 'stands in the knowledge of God'; and this knowledge is not discursive but 'of the heart,' a superrational intuition, direct, synthetic, and timeless."[7]

Thus, it seems pretty well agreed that peakers are meant to bring would-be peakers along. Indeed, if you do not have the experience of transcendence, how would you even be seriously motivated to enhance the probability that others would achieve such a state? Continuing along with Huxley in his Introduction to the Bhagavad-Gita, he assesses the impact of industrialization on religious education. His critique states: "External circumstances came to be regarded as more important than states of mind about external circumstances, and the end of human life was held to be action, with contemplation as a means to that end. These false and, historically, aberrant and heretical doctrines are now systematically taught in our schools and repeated day in and day out by those anonymous writers of advertising copy who, more than any other teachers, provide European and American adults with their current philosophy of life. And so effective has been the propoganda that even professing Christians accept the heresy unquestioningly and are quite unconscious of its complete incompatibility with their own or anybody else's religion."[8]

Although Huxley made this observation around forty years ago, I fear it is still all too true. And while it is true that Chardin's *Phenomenon* is dedicated "to those who love the world," as I understand this love of the world it is meant to be a love spawned of the realization that the world can lead us to God. This is one of the reasons why I will argue later for career education as part of religious education. For it is in *working* in the world that persons meet the maker of the universe in themselves. How wonderful, how lovely of the world to provide us with this opportunity and all these resources.

Jim, I realize that this letter is really getting long, and I am tempted to break now and start a new one to handle both additional observations on behavioral objectives and to discuss career education. But I think I will plow right on. At the same time I realize that what I have said above may come across as being a rebirth of "holier than thou" attitudes, the last thing we need.

On second thought, there is not much of a chance that that will result. My experience with those who have participated in the peak experience is that they are humble and unassuming. Nor do they necessarily go around advertising, willy nilly, this gift. Rather, as if taking a cue from the Cabbalah they are rather quiet and reserved in their general demeanor, "economically" dispensing their energies and guarding the stored treasure of grace which God has given them. Indeed, they are often content to disseminate their experience through poetry, painting, music, etc., or in quietly going about their daily routine in a manner so elegantly simple that the message, once received, hits the viewer like a bomb.

The fact that there are many people like this around encourages me in my efforts to see the transcendental experience made the focus of religious education. And the fact that many modern-day seekers can be found experimenting with newly formed or ancient religions of Eastern persuasion should but cause the Western religions to ask themselves if Huxley was perhaps correct about their unconscious heresy. If he was correct, then perhaps the effects of industrialization, i.e., huge corporations and monolithic bureaucracies, might be viewed as the problem in the culture rather than as the dispensers of vital services. These dysfunctional effects of industrialization have occasioned the rise of the new religions where the transcendent state figures centrally. What adjustments must be made to bring this mystical state front and center *again* in *our* religious bureaucracies?

BEHAVIORAL OBJECTIVES

Regarding further thoughts on behavioral objectives, I think I should first point out that I originally abhorred the notion. "Never," thought I, "would Socrates use them." And yet, it was you who once remarked in one of your seminars at Notre Dame that Bloom's *Taxonomy*[9] would probably rank with Plato's cave as a real contribution to education. Twenty years later I finally agree. But it took me many years, lots of experience, and even some writing back and forth with Ben Bloom himself to come to my present state of admiration.[10]

Still, what I fear about behavioral objectives is the way that people have a tendency to implement them. I attest to the common, everyday experience that human goals *emerge* as humans "interact." Nothing should interfere with such a flow of developing ends and aims. It's what all the fun is about. And yet, for purposes of better communication and for increased effectiveness and efficiency (including self esteem), the implementation of behavioral-based instruction seems to be a matter of reasoned good judgment. But, if they are implemented as hard-and-fast, fixed-in-concrete targets of action, if they are rigidly maintained to the detriment of spontaneity, especially if they are "mandated," they are not my cup of tea. If they are posed as a ready source and process for teachers to take advantage of, I think they will thrive in any educational setting including religious education.[11]

But perhaps there is one reason why behavioral objectives should be more at home in religious education than in public or private secular education. The nature of religion itself and of the religious experience is so intensely individual, that the only way to go about it is through differential, individualized instruction. Moreover, the highly personal and individual outcomes of religious education are ultimately wrapped up in the domain of values and nonlogical, intuitive grasping of the ultimate truth. Thus, a reading of Krathwohl's *Taxonomy of Educational Objectives; Affective Domain* by a conscientious religious education teacher should be, if it is presented properly, a marvelous occasion of self-revelation and even joyful appreciation of the underlying pattern of achievement plateus evident in values acquisition experiences.

For at the heart of any individualized delivery system of instruction must be detailed understanding of student achievement. Each student, at any period of his or her life, will vary in achievement in this nonlogical affective domain and it is nice to be able to ask some precise questions as to the students status and the "next best step" for the student. Both the precise questions and the desirable next-best-step behavior are available in the affective taxonomy.

I have written a small book on these "performance objectives" for the New York City Board of Education. It is bogged down seriously in the editing process—a not uncommon bureaucratic snafu.[12] Actually, I am not too anxious to have the book see the light of day. Although a few of my students and I are pleased with it, we still find it is a teacher turn-off. It seems the simplified system I have developed for the statement of the objectives is still a bit too rigid, ultrascientific, and unteacherly.

In addition, while I have erred somewhat in my presentation of the approach in the Board of Education book, I think our large systems have erred in their implementation. What is the essence of the mistake? Whatever it is, it cannot be the objec-

tives themselves, nor can it be their potential for individualization. The problem seems to be in their "marketing." I remember discussing the *Fleishman Report* on education in New York
State with Frank Keppel, late at night in our Fifth Avenue of-
fices. What we agreed upon, and what he put in the report,
was the suggestion that the behavioral objectives approach
should be supported by experimental research but should in
no way become a matter of public policy. Of course, only
months later New York State bureaucratically mandated the
objectives for the whole state at all educational levels. At last
count, this misguided policy has been made law in more than
twenty other states. What a paper blizzard![13]

I certainly hope that the same will not happen in religious
education. What I have learned where I have been successful
in bringing them into a teachers' day-to-day instruction is:

a. Proceed slowly.
b. Have teachers work in teams if they are interested.
c. Begin a "bank" of objectives for general use.
d. Don't fuss about the level of specificity in the statement.
e. Do stress the focus on student rather than teacher or
   curricular behavior.

Proceeding along the lines indicated has led me to considerable success with my students who are practicing teachers in
the New York City Public Schools, for the most part.

The Affective Domain

Finally, I think that if I wanted to interest religious education
teachers in behavioral objectives, I would facilitate their form-
ing a study group and begin, probably, with the affective domain. A little bit of the *Taxonomy* goes a long way, and I would
keep the sessions short and lively until they picked up the ball

themselves. In effect, what one would be doing in most cases is starting the teachers at awareness (1.0 on the affective taxonomy) of the taxonomic approach to religious affective learning. Where I indicated they might take up the ball, I mean one would be moving them to responding behaviors such that they as teachers voluntarily run their own sessions and develop their own implementation plans (2.0 on the taxonomy). Next, it seems desirable for them to place a value on this approach so that is consistently seen as useful, up to a point (3.0 on the affective taxonomy). Next, hopefully one would bring them to placing the approach in their value systems such that they would know when to use it and when not to use it and when they were misusing it (4.0 on the taxonomy). And, finally, it seems appropriate to have a few of them at least become characterized (5.0) on the taxonomy as the teachers who use behavioral objectives most of the time—i.e., real Bloomites, I call them. Note however that individual teachers are very different in their styles and some never will, nor should they ever be forced to, use the approach.

Well, that is all I have to say about behavioral objectives per se. What they mean for individualization is very important. Therefore, they are important for religious education, which is intensely individual; the problems we have with them are more a matter of the way we implement them than a matter of their intrinsic characteristics. Moreover, religious education teachers, if correctly exposed to the *affective taxonomy*, should embrace it, if not for its rigorous system, for its thoughtful insight into the growth of religious character. The approach can, in other words, "psyche out" the case history of every student in the religious education setting as to his or her awareness of transcendental experience (1.0), the response to make (2.0), the value such experiences have (3.0), the place in a hierarchy of individual values these experiences hold (4.0), and the status of this individual in light of the ultimate objective of making him or her a lifetime peaker (5.0).

In reviewing everything I have said so far about behavioral objectives, I realize that I have not really said what I think their greatest contribution to religious education can be. True, they can help bring about a sense of achievement, they can individualize, etc., but as I review my own experience with them and the failure to get them used voluntarily by teachers, I realize that Socrates *would* use them and *would* be quite comfortable with the taxonomies. "Know thyself," he used to say. Indeed, perhaps the greatest thing about both the cognitive and the affective taxonomies is the power they have to help a teacher know herself or himself. And perhaps this is the step missing in our efforts to get them used.

Up to now, education professors seem to have introduced the taxonomies to teachers as if they sprang brand new from the pen of some University of Chicago researcher. What's more, we seem to have assumed that we knew what their prime benefit would be in the instructional process. Curiously, we have never stopped to ask teachers how they see them being used. Speaking now as a teacher (as I have tried to do throughout these letters), I think I can safely attest to the taxonomies' power to let me see more clearly what I am doing when I teach. Their real value to me has not been in helping me to shape objectives (I don't) but in helping me to know myself and the process I go through with my classes. Their real import to me is, then, in the self-knowledge they enable me to attain by their use in my own thinking and my own spiritual development as a teacher.

It seems to me, as one last final point, that behavioral objectives will enter the lists of religious educational challenge when and only when some similar personal, "consciousness raising" experience is had by religious education teachers with the taxonomies, vis à vis their own behavior. And perhaps this raised teacher consciousness is more important than neat, detailed objectives and performance specifications. Perhaps, rather than telling teachers how to use the taxonomies, we should let them tell us.

The length of this letter is becoming awkward. What's more, something has happened that prompts me to end it here and save the treatment of the "career-prehensive" curriculum for religious education for the next chapter. The Egyptian project is hot! By that I mean that the proposal I wrote to set up a Career Experience Center in Egypt is alive and well after months of what I thought was delay signifying failure of the proposal to hit home. If all goes as planned, I leave for Egypt on April 15. Nevertheless, whether I go or not, I'll end this letter here, tell you more about Egypt in the next letter, and hopefully summarize in a very practical, here-and-now way, what all this emphasis on the social sciences can mean in day-to-day religious education.

I realize that this leaves you with an editorial problem . . . well . . . what did you expect? I think we can probably handle it with footnotes so as not to destroy the flow of the letters as they are written. But I am having other footnote problems and I hope to see you here in New York. As per your last telephone call, I hope you, Marlene, and James V will be visiting before the month is out. Which reminds me, I owe that young man a baptism present.

LOVE TO EVERYBODY,

Notes to Letter IV

1. The model as presented here is simplified somewhat from its basic presentation, which is found in Jacob W. Getzels, James M. Lipham, and Roald F. Campbell, *Educational Administration As a*

Social Process: Theory, Research, Practice (New York: Harper & Row, 1968), p. 105. The omnipresence of this model in much of the educational literature attests to its scholarly virtue and its practical ramifications.

2. What Dermit Kehoe originally did was see his own shift from Roman Catholicism to Anglicanism analytically, as an increase in the influence of the bottom half (i.e., the personal) of the model in his own experience in organized religion. It was when he saw the utility of the model to visualize and help him conceptualize his own behavior that he developed the idea to analyze *The Acts of the Apostles* with the model. At this point he pointed out, in justification of his choice of topic for his project, that the *Acts* were the report of the "institutionalization" of the church and thereby might be particularly susceptible to analysis by the Getzels model. His "hunch" proved quite correct.

3. Thomas J. Sergiovanni and Fred D. Carver, *The New York Executive: A Theory of Administration* (New York: Harper & Row, 1980), p. 53.

4. The reference here is to one of Chester Barnard's most difficult tenets, i.e., the definition of efficiency as *satisfaction,* instead of *getting something done in the fastest and cheapest way.* Further discussion of this point awaits a more management-oriented treatise, but it seems useful to point out that *satisfaction* in Barnard (i.e., his *efficiency*) is satisfaction of individual motivations and needs. Without such satisfactions, persistence of cooperation collapses, At the risk of overstatement and without detailed backup, I am suggesting here that the *satisfaction* alluded to by Barnard includes the satisfaction of all needs on the Maslow hierarchy. That this is so can be related ultimately to the functioning in his theory of a transcendental "sense of the whole" as we indicated above (page 59). Indeed, the presence of the transcendental experience in organized life can be shown to be the "ultimate" motivation available to executives in elliciting the most difficult and crucial contributions to an organization, i.e., in achieving peak efficiency.

5. See above, p. 46.

6. These "harsh" views on the "human relations" approach re-

ceive some support in Sergiovanni and Carver, *The New School Executive*, pp. 20, 88. At the same time this book's suggestion of a human resources model of administration would seem to be most worthy of consideration aimed as it is at professional and personal achievement of teachers.

7. Aldous Huxley, Introduction, in Swami Prabhavananda and Christopher Isherwood, translators, *Bhagavad-Gita* (New York: The American Library, 1956), p. 15.

8. Ibid., p. 17.

9. Benjamin S. Bloom. J. Thomas Hastings, George F. Madaus, *Handbook of Formative and Summative Evaluation of Student Learning* (New York: McGraw-Hill, 1971). I cite this work instead of the original taxonomies since it has a more applied approach. The summary in this work of the two taxonomies on pp. 270–277 and the presentation of the affective considerations on pp. 228–230 are particularly helpful.

10. The truth is that Professor Bloom was one of the people who interviewed me for my original staff position (i.e., staff associate) at the University of Chicago. In fact, however, I never took any of his courses and was at that time quite turned off by the whole approach, especially its quantitative and statistical side. The position on the use of the taxonomies I am taking in this letter attests to a complete about-face, in their regard, on my part.

11. This common-sense view of the spontaneity of the flow of means-ends changes in human action seems to me to be attested to, from a scholarly point of view, in Talcott Parsons, *The Structure of Social Action*, 2nd edition (New York: The Free Press, 1966). Moreover, the extreme fixation on the precise, detailed statement of learning objectives also seems to be not too far removed from the effects of what Whitehead called "the fallacy of misplaced concreteness" to which Parsons refers frequently.

12. The simplified approach to the shaping of objectives I devised for the New York City Board of Education can be found in the current edition of *Minimum Learning Essentials* in science, math, etc., published by the New York City Board of Education in 1979. The Introduction in each of the volumes includes the work I did to provide

faculties with a simpler but still substantive behavioral framework, providing fewer behaviors and optional degrees of specificity of statement of objectives.

13. I recount this episode to provide yet another instance of bureaucratic insensitivity to the realities of education, prestigious statements and reports to the contrary. This event took place about eleven years ago and is also further proof of my early reluctance to embrace the approach across-the-board.

14. I strongly believe that only teachers can tell us what all our educational research is about. Unfortunately, to date we do not have a way for teachers (as teachers) to speak out on exactly what shines and what doesn't shine as far as research goes. In effect then, what we need is a way for teachers (as teachers) to establish and define the research base of the profession, without interference from either researchers or bureaucrats.

Letter V

May 31, 1981
Feast of the Transportation
of the Prophet to Heaven
Cairo, Egypt

Dear Jim,

Lots have happened since the last letter. First of all, I am writing this letter from the front seat of a Chevy van somewhere in this wonderful city of Cairo. My companions are from the University of Zagazig—Mahrous Samak and Farag Gabal; the former, Zagazig's public relations man for the career education project and the latter our incredible driver. I am optimistic that we will be able to get the Career Experience Center underway in the next few months.

I have fallen in love with Cairo, the desert, the Egyptians, and I will continue this letter back in my room.

* * *

The Giza pyramids are outside my window. I have yet to see the Sphinx. You told me once that the Sphinx is the most haunting man-made artistic creation you ever saw in your life. I have taken in old Cairo, Coptic churches, Greek Orthodox sites, the citadel with the Mohammed Ali mosque. At the mosque, Mahrous and I discussed Islam and Christianity. Later, over coffee at the Tower of Cairo, he said that if Christ was God then he (i.e., Mahrous) himself was also God. Brilliant, no? By the way, how could Teilhard de Chardin have dismissed Islam so easily?

I guess we'll have to consider this letter an "extra." I know I have to present my version of a career-oriented religious education experience, as well as try to summarize the foregoing discussions of the social sciences and their implications for religious education. At the same time, surrounded by this incredible artistic heritage, I'll try to ease you and our readers into the next letter which, albeit later than anticipated, will deal with art and religious education.

But, before I forget, thank you for taking me to Nirvana. I went back a bit later in the week for dinner and decided that you had really found a great restaurant. As for Marlene, I know how you searched the globe for her and I know all your efforts were worth it. And, as for James V, what can I say? He is a delightful luncheon companion and I certainly am looking forward to many similar experiences. I hope you and your family can get to New York again very soon. Now back to Cairo and the tasks at hand. And to get us back on track, here is a poem that I wrote a year ago.

DEEP CREEK LAKE

OR

ON THE BACK OF ROMANS VIII

The desert . . . sands
the lake . . . waters
the juxtaposition . . . alters
the crinkles . . . crevice
the ripples . . . psalters
its just a possession
loss of which is a funny thing
which grows more every day

but every day becomes
easier to bear.

"I think men should touch more"
"I went to my daughter's wedding in a wrinkled dress"
(her husband forgot his teeth . . . her mother had just died)
wrinkled, rippled desert waters
wedding dress at altar
alludes the union of
Christ and his church.

In Egypt, the Nile becomes its
bank
and in Garrett County, Deep Creek
the lake becomes the shore
and above both, the sky permits the variegated interaction
with the past which allows the
bastard apostle to speak to us
now through the stars

It's day
not night
but this past is in both
albeit the veil of light permits us
to forget the presence of the past daily
but at night . . .
as we look up, we look ago . . .
long, long ago and join one in
an endless journey in
becoming neither . . .

> here nor there
> male nor female
> rich nor poor
> high nor low
> present nor future

The wave-hover water skier
skips the wake from swell to swell
of mysterious support
trailing a spray of peacock proud
water tail advancing into the
receding unfingered roseate
sunset skyrise
said the Psalmist's psalter . . .
"He told me it would be painful"
"I asked if I could remain lukewarm
a little longer"
"He told me to reach out more"

Four bottles of wine later, the
lake-set agape over, the
accomplishment was barely lessened
by the failure of the machines at
the end of this mechanical age
Having slipped delicately but deliberately into the depths
off the pier
the reading glasses settled into
scuttling along the rocks of the lake floor.

* They say: "Christian Dior" . . .
almost
And with the height of fashion at the
rock bottom
we wondered at our own wonder
and went to bed to dream of
    —carrying the cross
      —androgenous sex
        —undesired but deserved promotions
          —giving information
            —elaborate voter preparation
              —proudly displayed erections

only to awake
with a firmer sense of the allusion
of this promised land to the
real kingdom which fame not
humiliation ("Halfway to heaven"
said Mother Seton) can reveal, can
take away.

The poem is an effort to recount my sharing in a religious education series[1] run by Fr. Paul Byrnes in the mountains of western Maryland. As you can see, even then Egypt and the beautiful Nile were on my mind.

This simple little religious exercise consisted of a number of adults from the local summer community of Deep Creek Lake[2] coming together once a week for several weeks sharing with each other their experience in integrating their religious (in this case St. Paul's version of Christianity) experience and their everyday at-home and on-the-job experience.

SOCIAL SCIENCE SUMMARY

I found in this experience a kind of summary statement of the practical effects of bringing the social sciences to bear on religious education. First of all, the discussions always involved bringing to bear analytical frameworks from psychology, sociology, etc. on the text at hand and its meaning. Second, if you want to meet one satisfied religious education teacher you should meet Fr. Paul. As a result of his own satisfaction, he is able to afford the deepest satisfactions to his learners, in this case adults. Third, almost to a point too much for me the exercises are paced with each section having its clearly delineated task and its precise statement of objective. Finally, the group members constantly interrelated with each other, sharing each others' experiences at home and at work, meeting (a la Maslow) the need to interact so as to move on to a firmer sense of self and thence to the peak experiences, God willing.

With this little summary of our foray into the social sciences, proffered humbly, I'll move now to a discussion of what I think is the overall implication of the social sciences for religious education, i.e., ultimate . . . beyond satisfying the teachers, using precise behavioral objectives, etc. I am referring to what I would call a career-prehensive curriculum in religious education.

CAREER-PREHENSIVE CURRICULUM

The link between religious education and the workplace has occupied us before in this series of letters. Practically speaking, the significance of the common theme of transcendence (theoretically) between the workplace and religion gives us a strong theoretical base from which to argue for career-oriented religious instruction. With the mystic state functioning so centrally in both, not to take advantage of the juncture—at least to the point of serious exploration of its significance—would seem to me to be unconscionably mindless. Indeed, just as religion should look to the workplace for ways to improve itself—including its "delivery"—conversely the workplace might well look to religion to discover or rediscover its own commonalities with the "divines" of society.

I think everybody knows pretty well what a career is, as elusive as one is for so many people these days. The word *prehensive*, however, needs a little explication. I am using the word as Whitehead used it in *Science and the Modern World.*[3] The word alludes to the phenomenon that a whole is always greater than the sum of its parts. And a prehensive curriculum is one made up of elements, selected by the teacher, which go to make up, at the teachers professional judgment, a "whole" package for delivery to the student. But what are the elements of the prehensive curriculum I am talking about?[4]

Well, they are the elements included in instruction which are included on the basis of what we know from the social sciences. The first element of the instruction, is, then, the satisfaction of the teacher. In making this seemingly common-sense point, I think you will note that I am suggesting a change in the classic Tyler model of curriculum.[5] Without going into all of its admirable details, I think we can say that whatever curriculum is to be developed, according to the Tyler model, we are led to consider

    a. the requirements of the subject matter (e.g., religion)
    b. the needs of the student (e.g., motivation)
    c. the needs of society (e.g., economically viable persons)

You will note that in this most pervasive Tyler model of curriculum the personal needs of the teacher are nowhere, either accidentally or systematically, taken into consideration. This is a great omission if we are to take heed from the social science research on satisfying workers. Unless these teacher needs are taken into consideration and met, we can not even hope for effectiveness and efficiency.

And so among the elements of the prehensive instruction I argue for are the classic three elements of Tyler and the additional, and primarily important one, of meeting teacher needs.

Now, when I bring this point to my students in *public* education, they never really get the point until I suggest that this means that in any educational situation, administratively considered, the most important person is not the student, and certainly not the administrator; but is—and here's the point—the teacher.

Having thrived for some twenty years in public education glutted, almost, with the rhetoric of "meeting student needs," I find that the greater such rhetoric, the less productivity we get with the students. Something has been amiss. What has been amiss is the fact that in our running of education we have consciously or unconsciously neglected to satisfy our teachers. The results are easily predicted from social science worker and organization research.

In the religious setting, then, if we are to increase our effectiveness and efficiency, we must consider the most important person in that setting to be not the principal, not the assistant principal, not the pastor, not the curates, not the minister, etc., but the teacher.

I use the word career-prehensive to emphasize this point. For the career-prehensive curriculum proceeds in full acceptance of the assumption that the most important career of all is that of teaching. It is after all the career which is societally located to introduce others to all the other careers. If this does not happen, then adjustments must be made so that it will. Christ, after all, did not say, "Go out and say Mass"; rather, he said, "Go out and teach." A career-prehensive curriculum in religious education, then, is one which, in its design to meet the teacher's needs, focuses specifically on meeting the career needs of teachers, i.e., the needs which if met will lead to increased productivity.

Again, thanks to the social sciences we know what those needs are. They are not needs for affiliation or even for huge doses of material goods. They are needs for self-esteem, self-respect, pride in accomplishment, stature in the community as crucial to the success of the community, etc.

The career implications of this curriculum also add more elements to the instructional mix. They are:

  –the melding of "academic" and "vocational" learning
  –the melding of instruction with guidance and counseling
  –the use of community and family as partners in instruction

In these latter three elements, I am summarizing what I think is the result of the relatively recent thrust on a national level to enhance career education. The implications for religious education are great.

I think that the addition of these elements to the religious education mix will see fewer and fewer Sunday School *classes* and more and more *explorations* of "the realworld" prompted by the religious education teacher. But you say, can one really learn, let us say, about religion and still have a career orientation in the prehensive mix? I would say that in most cases, unless the career education is there, the instruction will fall flat. Which way is it better to learn about Christian charity? Is it better to sit in a class and read Saint Paul or is it better to visit the local firehouse with your religious education students to find out what is going on there and whether or not it is in any way prompted by religious principles? The answer of course is that neither way, at least as presented, is acceptable. There must be both of these components. The reading of Paul on charity combined with the firehouse trip would, it seems to me, bring the lessons of the epistles more clearly and emphatically to aspiring, impressionable minds. At the same time the whole notion of a career in the public service can be approached as a viable way to apply the canons of Christian charity to one's own life.

The mixing of guidance and instruction is an element that simply indicates that self-awareness, educational awareness, etc. must be outcomes of all instruction. In the constant decision-making process of students as they jockey their way into their societal roles, the teacher must constantly afford support to enhance this delicate and critical process. And the final career element, that of using the community and family as partners in instruction, is evidenced in our firehouse example above. Children, as John Dewey said many years ago, and all of us learn from growth-oriented experience of real life.

I think I would like to close this discussion of the career-prehensive curriculum in religious instruction with some further comments on the melding of academic learning with vocational learnings. As I indicated above, teaching is the most important career, for it is the career which has within it the power to introduce all the other careers to the student. Now, most teachers, and perhaps religious education teachers more so, have little experience in the world of 30,000 job titles that surrounds them. How then can a teacher who wants to teach, for example, *meditation techniques* do so with serious career ramifications?

The very thought of meditation brings me back to these wonderful Egyptians with whom I have been spending time. Indeed, the very feast which was celebrated on the day of my arrival has within it the name of one of the fifteen clusters of occupations, i.e., transportation. You see, as you well know, those 30,000 job titles out there (that it is the responsibility of the teacher to introduce to her or his students) have been categorized by the Department of Labor and the Department of Education (it looks like there will still be one in spite of the new administration) into fifteen *clusters* which constitute a kind of shorthand for use in instruction. But I am sure that this fast leap into the world of careers might be considered cavalier or semantically superficial so I had better back up a bit and come at this in a more normal instructional mode. Nevertheless, I hasten to add the topic of meditation is certainly at home in this land with these ancient peoples. The omnipresence of mosques throughout the city is evidence enough of the invitation to meditation which Cairo affords even the new visitor.

Now, one good way to have your students accept the seriousness of meditation techniques is to introduce them to people who take it seriously. Certainly the teacher himself or herself is a valuable role model for students in this regard, but, as is usually the case for students anyway, the grass is always greener. And so perhaps a trip to the United Nations is called for with a special attention paid to the interdenominational chapel. Perhaps, given the fact that we all can't live in New York, a visit to a local health club is called for where, increasingly, Hatha Yoga techniques are being taught. Then, too, perhaps "right in your own back yard" you will find the phys. ed. department or the football team practicing Transcendental Meditation, Hatha Yoga, or some other method to induce tranquility of mind. Then again, children's parents may be into jogging, and—as is the case with acquaintances of mine—the achievement of the transcendent state after a prolonged period of jogging would be a good, "grabbing" way to show students the presence and desirability of meditation and various meditative techniques in everyday life.

But what has all this to do with careers? Everything. For the real "meditators" that you visit or that visit your class are all employed and have probably embraced their own particular style of meditation because of aspects of their role in the world of work which call for them to transcend the day-to-day "grind" and to experience the satisfaction and strength that comes from experiencing oneself as part of something larger in the significance of which the individual can share. The meditating business executive can expose the students therefore to the thousands of jobs in, let us say, the *communications* cluster. The meditating airlines pilot or mechanic can increase students' awareness of the importance of contemplation in the *transportation* cluster. The coach and his athletes can increase student interest in the many jobs in the *hospitality and recreation cluster.* Only if students see meditation and its various techniques as a real part of real life, a part that is part and parcel of the way in which they will be able to meet their own needs for security and biological well-being, will the teachers task of moving students from 1.0 on the affective domain (i.e., awareness) to 5.0 (characterization by a value) be natural, easier, and more reliably effective. This is not to say that every class doesn't have a few "classic" sedentary mystics lurking toward the back of the room, so to speak, but even they will profit from the natural flow of instruction which melds traditional academic learning (e.g., meditation techniques, principles of charity, etc.) with career orientation, using especially the community as a partner in instruction.

As I develop the art and science letters for you, Jim, a further more complete and perhaps more systematic picture of the career-prehensive approach to instruction in religious education will emerge. For now, I hope you can see that the nature of such an approach calls first for meeting the needs of the teachers so that they can, confidently and with a sense of self-esteem, select elements of instruction in such a way that a titration point is reached, a new "curricular package" is readied and delivered for purposes of increased effectiveness and efficiency in religious instruction. In this case, the teacher 1) selects the topic based on his or her own needs, the needs of society, the needs of the student, and the needs of the subject matter itself. Then the teacher 2) melds in aspects of the career world which have a "goodness of fit." 3) Finally, the teacher, mindful of the developmental processes occurring in the spiritual and career development of the students, brings in the community to share in the act of the delivery of the career-prehensive package. Later on, consideration of art and science will afford the "prehensive" teacher with additional elements to be added to the instructional mix.

DOWN WITH SNOBBERY

Before leaving these career considerations and their implications for religious instruction, in case the kind of "snobbery" which acts to the detriment of public education should still be flourishing in religious education circles (i.e., the snobbery that would have academic education superior to career or vocational), let me add that Benedict early on pointed out that "to work is to pray." While it is true that states of transcendence can hit at any time and that we seem to play up the times when we are engaged in seemingly solitary activities, the true nature of the transcendent experience calls for it to occur more often than not at any time one is engaged in living and working. While the monk in his room is one way to model meditation, it would probably be better to model that monk fixing the community jeep with the "cellular" meditation a culmination of his engagement with the carburetor which, having flooded, made his superior late for an important meeting with the bishop. Therein lie the seeds of contemplation which, it is true, may grow and bloom in solitary meditation but more often then not, like Brother Leo and his pots and pans, flourish in the experience of life in a well-chosen, well-spent career.

Then, too, the career approach is evident in the parables of Christ. The sower, shepherd, etc . . . these are careers and people of Christ's time related to them. People have not changed in this regard, although careers certainly have!

Finally, the career orientation of religious education is a moral imperative. I know that every flea thinks he has the best dog in the world, but once you have seen the power of a career-prehensive curriculum delivered well, it seems to me you have little choice but to go and do likewise in whatever instruction you would engage in at any level.

Art and Transcendence

The last part of this letter, as promised, will introduce the notion of art and transcendence. Certainly my recent trips to the Islamic Museum, the Egyptian Museum, the Pyramids, etc. have stoked the fires for this one. But I think I'll confine my introductory remarks to two earlier personal experiences which are my own testimonial to the power of the arts in the spiritual development of people. I'll start with the latter of the two "memories."

I remember walking with you once on the Notre Dame campus and discussing with you my impending visit to the International Foundation for Advanced Study in California where I was to be administered a "massive" dosage of LSD, braced, so to speak, with psylocybin and mescaline. Years of preparation for the experience can be documented and its scientific propriety is still, I believe, considered excellent. It remains the first and only time I have ever used these drugs. You were, as I recall, neither unsupportive nor overly-supportive. You simply pointed out the fact that I was about to engage in something which heretofore had been on the periphery of most people's experience and indeed, it seemed safe to say at the time, something which had not, as near as you could tell, entered the campus environs of Notre Dame itself. And, you will recall it was upon my return from the experience that you set the wheels in motion for my entering the doctoral program at the University of Chicago.

The details of the experience under drugs are too voluminous to include here—and perhaps anywhere, being not only voluminous but exceedingly personal. One detail, however, is unforgettable. It was at the beginning of the experience itself, immediately following the administration of the drugs. All of a sudden I became a Jackson Pollack painting. Once having identified myself with the painting, the dribs and drabs of paint began to be removed from the painting in the reverse order of the way they had been applied to the canvas. In short, I was beginning to experience a classic (i.e., drug-induced) unpeeling of self-attributes leading me to the nothingness that is prerequisite to rebirth. Put another way, I was slowly dying as a painting. Because of my excellent preparation by excellent teachers and gurus for the experience, I was able to let this altered state of consciousness progress at its own speed and method to the point of nothingness whence I sprang to my new mode which I will not describe here.

The point is that the power of art in helping to understand one's own spiritual nature and development was so great (and still is with me) that it figured at the very outset of this drug-induced experimentation with altered states of consciousness.

While it came as somewhat of a surprise to me, on reflection many years later, my personal affinity for painting and transcendence was in evidence much earlier in my life. And that is the story of the second personal experience.

Next weekend, I will be leaving for the Midwest, where, toward the end of the month, June 27th to be exact, my godchild . . . my late brother's oldest daughter, Mary, will marry David Andrew Ferran.

As you know, all my family is special to me, but Tom's family (my late brother's family) is extra special for the obvious reason. Well, as was my wont, frequently over the years I would visit the folks in Kansas City, and invariably I would trek off to the Nelson-Adkins Museum with at least one or two of the kids in tow, or sometimes even with Carole, my sister-in-law. A few years back, Mary and her sisters Leslie and Laura cornered me in front of the museum and finally asked; "Uncle David, why is it that everytime you come to Kansas City to visit us we end up going to the museum?" My response surprised me, for I hadn't thought of the event which I recounted to them in many many years. You see when the good nuns of the Sisters of the Holy Humility of Mary were getting me ready for my first Communion, I must have asked what it was going to be like. And one of the sisters, probably Sister Mary Bernadette (first grade) or Sister Mary Florentine (second grade) must have told me that it was the most beautiful thing in the whole world. Communion would be the most wonderful thing I could think of. Well, I promptly envisioned myself all alone in a large room in a museum somewhere, free to wander, and wonder at my own speed and desire, from painting to painting. And so from a very early age the awareness of the religious affinities of the fine arts has been a part of me.

The next two letters on 1) art and 2) its implications for religious education spring from a very deep and personal side of me that I hope I will be able to convey. Even today, surrounded by the Promise Art Collection, small as it is, I still find myself wandering from painting to painting in a kind of wonder experience that I can't really describe. My friends and advisors will be quick to point out that the collection is, in the main, mystical and perhaps whimsically mysterious.

I probably won't get around to writing another letter until later in the summer. I promise to have the book to you in September . . . fingers crossed. And before our attentions go beyond this land of the Pharaohs, I'd like to pay it homage one more time by referring to a thought from a prominent Rosicrucian. The name of the Rosicrucian is Walter J. Albersheim.

I recently saw a letter from him to a Roman Catholic. In it he observed the similarity between the slain Osiris and the slain Christ. Long ago, our Egyptian friends knew that a God who suffers helps us to transcend our own suffering.

Farewell from the land of Osiris. Goin' to Kansas City.

LOTS OF LUV.
DAVID

Notes to Letter V

1. The series is: John Joyce, Project Director; Gerard Weber, editor, *Romans 8* (Santa Monica: Intermedia Foundation, 1979). As you can see, I got part of the title of the poem immediately above directly from the series. The lake setting, the people from the lake, this "with it" set of materials made for a wonderful and natural religious education experience.

2. By coincidence, Einstein once summered at Deep Creek Lake. Fr. Paul's house on the lake is across from the promontory where the great scientist used to enjoy what surely have to be the most spectacular night skies, filled with dazzlingly clear sights of stars, planets, falling stars, etc. We'll hear more about him when we talk about science and religious education.

3. Alfred North Whitehead, *Science and the Modern World* (New York: Mentor Books, New American Library, 1959), pp. 63, 67 ff.

4. I am starting to build here to a notion of a curriculum which has many elements, but whose essential nature consists only in the *probability* that certain elements will be in evidence over time. In other words, the career-prehensive curriculum, under observation, need not always show evidence of all the elements functioning simultaneously. Rather, each of the elements has a strong probability of being witnessed in any observed instruction, but its absence at any one point of time is to be expected. The curriculum I envision takes its cue from modern particle physics, especially a la quantum physics, which sees the universe as made up of constantly emerging and

disappearing particles whose behavior is far from determinate, a matter of probability. Thus, the prehensive curriculum consists of elements in a "mix" in which the hard-and-fast observable presence of each element is not only an unrealistic expectation but methodologically speaking a matter of quite determined indeterminacy. Looking at a curriculum this way seems to me to once again reflect the dynamic character of the teacher consciousness enmeshed in a constantly growing and evolving multidimensional matrix of means-ends chains. Further "fleshing out" of this curriculum remains for future letters.

5. Ralph N. Tyler, *Basic Principles of Curriculum and Instruction* (Chicago: University of Chicago Press, 1950).

Letter VI

July 3, 1981
Feast of Saint Thomas the
Apostle
First day of Ramadan

Dear Jim,

Writing on the Feast of St. Thomas, the doubter, seems somehow appropriate in a book developed within the context of faith, its development and sustenance. It's also the weekend of the Fourth of July which brings to mind Isaac Hecker's belief in the combined power of the church and America. Only time will tell.

The Cairo project is still alive and the new proposal went over to Zagazig by diplomatic courier last week.

The focus of this letter will be on the arts and their ramifications for religious education. This letter will be a mite theoretical, and I'll save the practical implications for the next letter. To start things off, here's a poem I wrote which seems to fit here because it "documents" two heightened consciousness moments of mine occasioned by arts experiences.

The Moon and No Sixpence

The finely attenuated conducting of the overture to
    Lohengrin
supported the director's arms on air solidified by
the poisonous sweetness of the Wagnerian airs evoking

reminiscenses of sensual delight craved but unattained
and peering from a pier the sky become the big
cloud and the cloud become the many layered lavered
    universe
in constant flux and wisping to so fine an
attenuation that its absorption into the cloud of the
sky went unnoticed by the poet nature-prone and park
    wondering
experiencing god once more not in one but between two
    flowers
if one can place god. And dream like the stigmata came
    even closer
signaling disappearance into the ultimate unity of the
    universal
cloud like the faun so perfectly executed that stillness
    achieved
by the dancer precipitated his disappearance into the stuff of
    the
ballet art. Indeed, where is the
figure and what does the ground look like if all is shifting so
    that
one at any time can be the other? How can all be fluxian
    change
if it all is changing so that there can be no passage from
permanence to permanence? This final corner into which
we all used to paint ourselves when young rhetoricians
did call themselves solipsists seems now to be important
only to have gone through it. Is it possible that the anguish
then experienced was a kind of redemptive act for the soul
    self
which now having rejected it all as ultimately meaningful is
    bored?

The opening lines refer to an experience I had during the overture to a Wagnerian opera at the Metropolitan. I have a pet theory that says if an art form is good and intense enough, it should jump, so to speak, into another art form.[1] I'm not sure if I can make this perfectly clear, but, for example, in this case the gorgeous Wagner music was so expertly conducted that the sound seemed somehow to be not only heard but literally *felt* and *seen* as "air sculpture." It was as if the excellence of the performance in sound extended itself beyond into sight so that the patently musical experience in sound became literally a visual experience of sculpted, felt air.

In the middle of the poem, there is a reference to a faun. It is the faun of Debussy's *Afternoon of a Faun* as executed by Peter Martins of the New York City Ballet. His art is of such under-stated, exceptional strength and intensity that, at the end of the ballet, as he came to his final rest, he literally disappeared into the overarching powerful "stuff of the ballet art." To me, this is an experience of experiencing with the artist the loss of self and the communion with the greater "something" . . . i.e. the ballet art.

I hope these two examples will show you why I am focusing on making religious education experience rich in arts experi-ence. Since I still continue to suggest that the purpose of re-ligious education is to enhance the probability that a person will experience transcendence, it must seem obvious that a form of human activity which deals daily with transcendence is a human activity most suitable for leading "students" to a better chance at achieving religious transcendence. Put an-other way, the experience in the arts is a rich source of oppor-tunities to provide students with altered states of consciousness and perception. A rich exposure to this human activity can certainly result in peak experiences, making them appear to be exactly what they are . . . i.e. perfectly natural occurrences which the soul needs for its satisfaction and well-being.

The first point I would like to make is that the arts have the capacity to show us that what we are experiencing in our everyday lives need not be all that there is. In addition, they can show us that past this everyday experience, just as "outside" Plato's cave, there is a "light," a force, a transcendent reality with which we can get in tune, so to speak. We can commune with this something "bigger than ourselves," if we but allow the arts to have their sway in our lives. Unlike Plato's vision of the "good," however, this transcendent experience is not reserved for the elite few destined to be rulers. Rather, these experiences of transcendence are increasingly made available to all through the radio, television, and other media. And the assumption of this increased media coverage of the arts is that the arts are for all the people.

Now, at this point in time it seems reasonable to assume that you might think me still "elitist" in spite of my protestations to the contrary. After all, to how many people is it given to regularly partake, in person, of the best that the arts have to offer such as a Peter Martins or a Met production of Lohengrin? And even if it is granted that media coverage of such events increases the audience, surely that audience must be of quite a cultured and sophisticated nature, primed, so to speak, to "get off" on the high culture proffered from super professional stages.[2] Indeed, it is difficult to see some of my friends who were former prison inmates experiencing transcendence through Lohengrin's overture when the disco around the corner is more to their liking. Ballet and Lohengrin are not everybody's cup of tea so to speak. So of course the transcendence-enhancing potential of the arts will vary from individual to individual, and, in all candor, the art available at the corner disco is more "accessible" for my friends fresh from prison.

And here a difficulty presents itself. There seems to me little doubt that the corner disco has the potential to introduce people to and sustain their enjoyment of an enhanced, transcendent state of consciousness. I'll develop this more later. Indeed, quite a bit of my poetry speaks to this point. Here's a sample, one poem of a quintet called the *Nutmeg Cycle*. I think it might help make the point. At the same time as we consider the local disco as an opportunity to commune with something greater than ourselves, we must not forget to note that the same place in many instances is rife with drug, alcohol, and other substance abuse. Well, here's the poem.

The Phenomenon of Nutmeg Metz:
The Return to the Cha Cha Palace

The good news of Christ's birth falls easily here
   on the ears of these unslaughtered innocents
the messiah's emergence at first in their midst they missed
   midst the bright lights and portents
of salsa and disco and Jo gyro go-go reflecting
   in faith sooth sans malice
and Nutmeg Metz gloried at being again with these
   Christ's least at ease in the hot Cha Cha Palace

The planetization through eucharist libation grows
   glowing through these boys and girls
their lack of real power embodies the shower of
   God's grace in tangential swirls
and radial twirls and their primary
   care in divine milieu fair's not the phallus
nor braless endowment but love-giving looks send
   balloons dancing through Cha Cha Palace

These love darts cementing the parts to the whole
   commodity sensual for trading

and popes, parents, pastors, and parents
    parading in vain render tender upbraiding
just leave them alone and like Nutmeg observe
    and delight in their sweet flesh gyrating
sustaining the dance of the transfigured
    matter and finally all demons sating

So sin disappears as the light-speckled air
    sweeps the floor vainly looking for flaws
and the music relaxes the uptight syntaxes of
    nerves tautly forming the craws
of poets and writers and doctors and
    waiters and honest transvestites with flowers
and quiet will soon seep with moonlight leap
    lightly to soften the sleep-children's hours

His corner of eye caught a smatter of light
    destined ever to fashion a sigh
from the heart of the Nutmeg who thought for a
    while it was Alice-O, why did she die?
but she didn't you know, she's just part of
    the flow of this motion entrancing unending
and the sigh-forcing lights are but mites of her
    soul flashing ever for Nutmeg transcending
                                            July, 1979

I think it might help you to know that the lead character,
Nutmeg Metz, has returned to this disco (called the Cha Cha
Palace) in hopes of reliving happier moments there
. . . moments when his girlfriend, Alice, was there with him.
Alice used to be a dancer there and she died, one night, in
Nutmeg's arms in the Palace. Over and above that, you proba-
bly can catch bits and pieces of Merton and Teilhard de Char-
din and a touch of Alfred Whitehead. Now these fellows might

seem an unlikely trio to be inhabiting the likes of a disco parlor, but, in truth, I find them all much at home there. First of all, Whitehead's old "saw" that *the whole is greater than the sum of its parts* helps to grasp the totality of the disco situation which has a power, especially over youth, that I still find difficult to cope with. And yet the titration-like addition of elements until that magic point of "freedom" is achieved is unmistakable when viewed through this Whitehead maxim. The combination of sound, light, movements, rhythm, etc. suddenly fashion themselves together in a being much more than any of the individual participants, and, while the scene is apparently suffused and diffused with sex of all kinds, the end result is that the sex itself becomes less significant than that to which it has been added as just one more ingredient. In effect, it, like all the other elements, is transcended.

Merton once referred to sexual attraction as a tradeable sensual commodity, and it is in this trading off of attractions that one sees the tangential energies of being to being exercised while at the same time radial energies direct the entire ensemble to a totality beyond any individual attraction, a la Chardin.

Perhaps this transcendental elan which I have found in the disco scene may appear to be naive, if not dreamily stupid, on the part of a would-be poet. Indeed, one lady friend, on reading the poetry, wanted to go immediately to the Palace. But another lady friend, upon reading the poetry, totally refused to accept the fact that I had ever really experienced any such thing in a real disco. Well, the fact is that the poem was written both as a result of some random disco experiences of mine combined with the stories my discophile friends would tell me about this or that fantastic evening at one of the posh, glamorous, and internationally famous discos that have regaled New York's "with it" set for the last few years. And so I do not think I am necessarily reading too much into the scene. All I am basically saying is that there is a disco art, and it is capable of bringing us to a state of altered consciousness, outside ourselves, beyond ourselves.

THE "IMMORAL ARTIST"

As to the drug, alcohol, and other substance abuse which one finds very often, but not necessarily, in the disco scene, I don't think I have to tackle at this time the problem of the immoral artist, a theological boondoggle for a long time before this. That this problem takes this form at this point in time should come as no shock. I have not read recently where Wagner's case for canonization has been pushed, and I know more than one musician who has relied on a chemical to get him through a gig. And without dodging this issue, but facing it, let me just refuse to judge it at this point in time. Holding such judgment in abeyance permits me to suggest that to many younger people the disco art form is a powerful attractor, and religious educators may take a cue or two from it if they would enhance their students' prospects of achieving mystical experience. If this sounds as if I find in the lights, sound, and movement of a disco the same elements as in the candles, organ, and ritual of a high church ceremony, then it is sounding the way I want it to. And just as candles, organs, and ritual are not to everyone's liking, so too is disco not to everyone's liking, but it is an option and a powerful one for the transcendent-bent religious educator. (Indeed, even with the young there is evident a cleavage between the discophiles and the rock-and-roll enthusiasts. The latter have even declared the death of disco!) Given that I have tried to demonstrate the enhancement of transcendence through the arts, it remains to point out that this transcendence can occur by the *performance* of the art as well as by the *appreciation* of the art.

ART PERFORMANCE AND APPRECIATION

Thus, religious educators would feel quite at home in facilitating the artistic *performance* of their students as well as the artistic *appreciation* of these same would-be peakers.

I am reminded again of the scene from the Bing Crosby, Ingrid Bergman flick, *The Bells of Saint Mary's,* in which the youngest children in the school are rehearsing a play about the birth of Christ. Sister "Ingrid" apologized to Father "Bing" and says: "I must tell you; the children have done this all by themselves. Every line they say is a surprise to me." Well put, sister! The art form in question is that of a play. The children are not there to appreciate it but to *do it.* And in the process they generate a spontaneous interest and insight into the religious learning at hand that is a source of constant surprise and delight to their mentors.

ARTISTS AS MODELS

And so art as *performed* and art as *appreciated* help to bring us closer to that state of consciousness outside ourselves, in union with something greater than ourselves. But there is another aspect of art which is crucial to understand if we are to use art to its fullest in our religious education quest.

Under consideration now is the fact that the artist is a nigh onto perfect model of devotion. The composer and conductor of Lohengrin, the ballet dancer, Peter Martins, the disco dancer (e.g., John Travolta) insofar as they achieve transcendental heights in and through their art can be studied and imitated in this regard. The training, study, and effort of a composer, conductor, ballet star, disco dancer, etc—these are aspects of life which are important for all to know about. For it is only with great work and dogged determination that the heights of artistic expression and experience are reached. Artist friends of mine come to mind readily. David Bruce Duncan, the collage painter mentioned in an earlier letter, will often times paint through the day and the night achieving the union with his art out of which come his important works. How many years of practice and determination did it take to bring Evan Paris, a young violinist friend of mine, to the point where he can arrive with his "fiddle" at a weekend retreat only to lose himself from one o'clock to five o'clock in the afternoon simply playing the violin? The creation of art is the creation of a state of enhanced consciousness, and it comes only with thorough preparation and persistence.

True, the reward of ecstasy can come at any time, and few if any would argue for a cause and effect relationship between any specific set of activities and the achievement of a peak experience. But the general pattern of work, great effort, persistence, and dedication is crystal clear as is its "reward." Certainly a similar pattern of behavior is indicated for those who would achieve to the heights of spiritual experience. While mystical experiences in a very real sense, like the wind, blow[3] where they will, the pattern of life which is conducive to their occurrences is like that of the artist, one of work, great effort, persistence, and dedication.

ART AND SELF ESTEEM

Another reason arguing for the inclusion of the arts in religious education curricula is the phenomenon, discussed in an earlier letter, of the lowered self-esteem which seems to be haunting our society, occasioned, as I suggested, by our massive, impersonal bureaucracies and corporations. The sense of individual futility, the inability to see oneself as creative and innovative in the scheme of things, and the general tendency to denigrate one's own efforts in the shadow of seemingly insuperable impersonal, death-to-spirit-dealing "management procedures" have left us all feeling a lack and a want in ourselves that leads us to substance abuse, therapists, analysts' couches and, in general, depression.

And yet each one of us is created in the image and likeness of the creator and each one of us is then, at least analogously, a creator. It seems as if I was raised on this truthful maxim, and yet as I look about I see us all encouraged to be anything else but creators. Rather, we are to fit into our impersonal niches and be grateful that we have such a niche. How curious it is that this docility is encouraged by individuals who call themselves administrators and governors. Curious, indeed, it is when you consider that, to Aristotle, government, i.e., management, administration, etc., is the highest *art*. But we need not rest in gratitude for all this mental midgetry pompously proffered as sound management techniques, if we but find within ourselves that creative spark with which and through which we can create.

Self-concept development has been a priority in public education since I entered its lists over twenty years ago. And yet I have really seen the best results in this priority where the arts were involved. For many years I worked as a volunteer and trustee of the School Art League in the city of New York. As the cutbacks hit and the arts were the first to get hit, I saw increasingly the importance of preserving the direct routes of artistic expression for our children. The League's annual awards ceremony at the Metropolitan Museum of Art was proof enough of the power of artistic achievement to brighten the eyes of students and teachers as well as make a trustee or two choke up with the beauty of the whole affair.

In still another national effort, the AGE program (the Arts in General Education) sponsored by the Rockefeller Foundation afforded schools and children the opportunity to integrate all the arts into every aspect of instruction. A visit to one of these schools was invariably a visit to an oasis of solid sense of self and solid sense of what education was all about. Here the arts were used not only as a means to self-expression but as a means to motivate, to make the instruction not just palatable but, oftentime, even fun for the student and for the teacher.

Edith Gaynes, a former executive director of the New York City Public Schools, used to say that the arts were the "rice and beans of education." The older I get, the more I know she was right. Without the arts, education in general is a dry and dessicated enterprise doomed to ineffectiveness and inefficiency. And yet, we seem to strip our schools of the arts the first time the budget appears to be the least bit precarious. Well, we should not be surprised at this since those budgets have gotten into the hands of people who, by nature and seemingly by profession, haven't the slightest idea of what a peak experience is. And even though they could directly correlate their slashing of the arts budget with the decline in scores, there is little hope of convincing this breed of bureaucrat that his or her priorities are way off.[4] The point I am making here is that any instruction must be rich in arts experiences if it is to be effective. This is true of public education and, a fortiori, is true of religious education . . . especially religious education, which is aimed at a state of consciousness so akin to the heights of artistic consciousness. For high self-esteem is necessary for achievement and hierarchically is a need which precedes that of transcendence. In my next letter I'll try to suggest some ways of making the arts a part of religious education as an extension of the notion of a prehensive curriculum for religious education.

ART AND ORGANIZED RELIGION

I have heard it said that art increasingly reflects deeply religious concerns when the societal mechanisms for the furtherance of religious concerns fail in their mission. Whether or not this is true for all time, I do not know. I do know, however, that my own familiarity with the contemporary art world leads me to agree with the observation, at least as far as my experience is concerned. I won't stop to document why I say this in any detail, but I would proffer the observation that a trip through contemporary galleries leaves one with the feeling that much of what is being produced has a very explicit concern for the transcendent (e.g., Richard Chiriani's landscapes), the mysterious (e.g., David Bruce Duncan's collages of his dreams) and the overtly religious nonrepresentational work of Archie Rand (the murals of the B'nai Josef Synagogue in Brooklyn). Granted that my selection of art and artists is necessarily influenced by my own interest in things of the higher consciousness sphere, still it can be granted that I have had no difficulty in finding works to suit my tastes and interests.

Along these same lines, in a recent book, *The Time Falling Bodies Take To Light* by William Irwin Thompson, the observation is made that, in the case of godless and nonreligious situations, perhaps the only way to approach people for purposes of enhancing their transcendental potential's actualization is through the arts. Thompson apparently can see in art in general, including the comporary scene, the introduction they afford to transcendental states of awareness. Moreover, if I understand him, he attributes to the arts the only real power available to someone who would wish to introduce a godless age to transcendence. While I do not agree that the arts alone are available for such purposes in such situations, I do agree that the arts do have this power.

ALL THE ARTS

And I hasten to add that this power is in all the arts. The first-act closing number of Duke Ellington's revival/review on Broadway, *Sophisticated Ladies,* is a case in point. Here the lighting, costumes, photography, music, lyrics, etc. all join together until at one point all the cares of the day seemingly evanesce into that universal something which I was able to share at a matinee two days ago with one of my YMCA colleagues, Ron Overton. Ron is a manager at the Magic Pan Restaurant. He is also a member of the board of managers of the Uptown YMCA. He had an extra ticket so I got a freebie to the matinee. We both observed that the final number of the first act had "it" much more than the final number of the second (and last) act. In the former, the arts elements in a wonderful prehensive mix congealed and coalesced until the effect was the realization that one was being transported somehow beyond the cares of the day, beyond the discipline of the individual arts, and beyond the individual talents, sexuality, skin color, ace bandages, etc. of the performers into a nameless but very real totality. No wonder they called him the "Duke"!

It occurs to me that examples like this may seem to some to be using a rather loose definition of the word, *art.* That is why I am using these examples. There is a tendency for people to think of the more "sophisticated," art forms and neglect the obvious crowd pleasers. Thus, I can imagine someone wondering at considering the last number of the first act of *Sophisticated Ladies* on a par with the quintet from *Der Meistersinger.* Well, I suppose a case can be made for the superiority of the art forms in opera as opposed to the art forms in musical comedy. But these considerations are irrelevant to this discussion. The function of the arts in religious education is to reach the learner. And the learner, in most cases, will not be found to be at the Wagner level,[5] whatever that may be. Rather, each learner will have an art form appropriate to his or her own needs dispositions. As John Dewey said so long ago, you have to start with the learner where he or she is, not where you would have him or her be.

Religious Antagonism to Art

For now, however, I thought I would close this letter with a discussion of religious antagonism to art. There are canons about the arts in many religions to the point where some religions go so far as to practically ban art from their physical premises. To these few religions, my letters will be of little consolation. I simply cannot agree. Their motivation, while construed from good intentions I am sure, seems too much like the current public school administrators who have decimated the art programs in our public schools in the name of getting down to the basics in time of economic crunch. But the arts are the basics! What good is it to be able to read *horse* if you have never seen one. Maybe, however, if you saw a picture of one, had the opportunity to draw one, or perhaps even got to play the part of one (either end), the reading of *horse* would be meaningful and unforgettable. It seems such common sense that it is so; I can say no more.

Still other religions, and important ones, put regulations on the use of art. Here, adjustments can be made. I am aware, for example, of the fact that representational art is forbidden in orthodox Jewish synagogues. Still, a friend of mine, in a well-recognized tour de force, has muraled, upstairs and down, the B'nai Josef Synagogue in Brooklyn—the second time ever such a feat was accomplished, the first being before Christ, in

Damascus. My friend's name is Archie Rand, and it is his genius to have executed a muraled synagogue reverently and *legally* by marrying the canons of ancient religion with those of modern, abstract art. What this says is that, where there are parameters set on the arts they can be worked with and within to achieve the kind of religious instruction we are advocating in these letters.

The B'nai Josef Synagogue is a must for you and Marlene on some future New York visit.

It's raining outside. What a terrible Fourth of July weekend this has been. I am just perverse enough to be one of those people who like rainy holidays. How else will I ever get these letters written?

My next letter, as promised, will deal with some practical implications of a healthy dose of the arts in religious education aimed at transcendence. As for the points I have tried to make in this letter, I would sum them up as:

- —The arts are valuable to religious education because they familiarize the learner with the altered state of transcendent consciousness.
- —The evil, immoral, or amoral ambiance of arts and artists is no reason to ignore their value for religious education purposes.
- —Arts as construed in these letters include music, dance, movies, etc.
- —In religious education, not only the *appreciation* of art but the *performance* of art is to be included.
- —The arts will enhance self-concept, a propaedeutic to peak experiences as well as day-to-day achievement.

I wonder what Saint Thomas Aquinas would say to all this.

As ever,
David

Notes to Letter VI

1. I can't resist observing that I find in this "jump" perspective on the relationship between two or more art forms more than a little flavor of the modern physics we'll deal with in later letters. For the "quantum" perspective in physics speaks to the "jumps" electrons (quanta) make from orbit to orbit on the basis of receiving or emitting more or less energy. And, if I understand all this correctly, the best we can do is to estimate the *crowd* behavior of electrons; in principle, we are consigned never to know exactly where any one particular electron will "light," so to speak. That is, we can't exactly predict, but only give the probability of, which orbit shell any particular electron will occupy in the future.

Similarly, we can't exactly predict when one art form will "jump" into another artistic art form. That, indeed, is half the fun of it. But in both instances, physics and art, it seems clear that sufficient energy will cause some quantum, *discontinuous* jump. And if after this discussion someone should simply observe that I had an overactive imagination and was not observing any such quantum jump, I am perverse enough to take solace in the new physics where the very reality of the jumping electrons in question is seen scientifically as, in some way, created by the scientific observer and the act of scientific observation itself. Is the electron really there without the observer? Is the shift from sound to touch really there without the arts consumer? Good questions, these, and worthy of further exploration.

Clearly, though, it does seem as if things do change discontinuously and things do as a function of energy jump about in relationship to one another. A discontinuous jump from sound to sight and touch, then, is not all that off-base. And, the observer, himself or herself, has much to say as to what will be seen and what will be experienced as jumping from being heard to being seen and felt, i.e., from music to sculpture.

2. This note, written much later than the letter in which it appears, can bear witness to the rapidly increasing amounts of arts entertainment occurring in television circles. Certainly the arts-rich Arts Cable productions are evidence of a new common-arts consciousness

which can be seen as truly emerging and truly providing religious educators with further reason to incorporate the arts into their instruction.

3. I hope I am not guilty of what you describe as the "blow theory" of religious education. I don't think I am. The unpredictability of the occurrence of my own peak experiences certainly doesn't call for me to lay back and wait for them to happen. Rather, a constant habit of active meditation seems to characterize my solitary times which is my way of seeking for more and more understanding and appreciation of myself and the transcendental experience. On the other hand, one can be "blown away" in the middle of a meeting in Washington during an experience that comes replete with vision. I won't recount, but just mention such an occurrence I can share. It is evidence to me that the unpredictability of the occurrence of altered states goes hand in glove with discipline and structure. They, like the movement of electrons and photons in subatomic particle physics, may have a disturbing random quality, but they are not experienced by randomly looking for them in haphazard style. Rather, as in the new physics, the "region of preparation" and the "region of measurement" are extremely structured—sine qua nons of the particles' detection. Even in the instance of de novo, chance, or serendipitous discoveries (e.g., the Curies and radium) the response is structured pursuit of its real meaning, not reliance on chance or serendipity.

4. I am aware of the fact that many of my bureaucratic friends, should they read these letters, will feel somewhat chagrined at my constant negative readout on them and their behavior. Surely they can easily accuse me of forgetting the political context of their decisions thereby exonerating them for the culpability of their follies. But I am not determining culpability . . . that's not my task here. It is quite possible that their degrees of freedom in setting their priorities are so minimal that the allocation of praise or blame in any such situation would be difficult. (Curiously, however, it can be observed that praise-taking is no great problem.) And I know such behavior is justified on the basis that one must "manipulate perceptions" of oneself to fit the up-tight, me-first situation in which many of my friends find themselves. But as I try to point out to my management

classes, such constant fictionalizing of perception is dangerous. One soon begins to believe one's own perception, the perception becomes internalized, and all too often one ends up being exactly what one set out, idealistically, to defeat. Moreover, the anxiety produced in an arena of praise and blame, where responsibility is impossible to determine, is the anxiety of an arena where only sociopaths can function effectively. And to my students and my friends I say, "Get out!" To stay is too risky to one's own well-being.

It can be observed that we have created organizations which reward those qualities we have always deemed the vilest. Such a situation is cancerous not only for society in general but for each of us as individuals.

Finally, it seems only honest to point out that I have known a *few* exceptions to the rule in this regard. Indeed, I have fond memories of one federal bureaucrat, so fine and sensitive that I still wonder at his achievement as a combination professional and bureaucrat. I have yet to find a satisfactory explanation of his behavior in the literature. Indeed, the literature regularly points up the contradiction between the bureaucratic and professional ethical codes.

5. Exceptions to the rule in this regard are, I feel, much more numerous than we normally assume. I am thinking of the case of a young man, not an ex-offender, having difficulty finding his personal rudder for schooling and career. With, as near as I can tell, no previous exposure, and equipped with weak writing and reading skills, this individual immediately became fascinated with Wagner's *Der Meistersinger* (especially the long boring parts!) as well as with Taylor's book on Greek philosophy. I mention this simply to indicate that assuming what level of arts appreciation an individual is at is a risky business; more often than not, I am impressed with what so-called slow learners can grasp most naturally and quickly.

Letter VII

DEAR GAMAL,

Thanks for your note. I am pleased to know what your name is in Arabic. You will be pleased to know that all daughters (Egyptian) referred to in your letter are still very safe, at least as far as I know. I will reserve further discussion of this topic (i.e., relationships and sex) until a later letter in which I'll take a few shots at bringing some of this thinking to bear on what is certainly a twentieth-century obsession . . . and maybe with reason.

While on the subject of things Arabic, I can report an experience I had in Cairo. As usual, its ineffable quality will make this report seem paltry and simple minded but such is the nature of the subject we deal with.

AN EGYPTIAN EXPERIENCE

One morning, my companion and driver picked me up in Giza and we headed for the center of Cairo. Suddenly, my entire surroundings were transfixed and the total realization of God's ultimate victory in all things overpowered me, jolting me into the realization that all my fretting and worrying about this and that were quite useless, silly, futile, etc. Naturally, after the experience passed, I went right back to fretting and worrying, but it is nice to know that the human condition now is not the human condition ultimately.

Bringing you up to date on a few things: The YMCA project to renovate the Holy Name Community Center is moving along. We are "in" for a quarter of a million dollars to refurbish the place (pool, gymnasium, classrooms, etc.) through the YMCA capital development drive which begins this year. If the archdiocese and we can come to terms, the project could see the light of day in a very little time.

I never did get to Kansas City. Priorities here have been so hectic that I cut the trip to the Midwest short with just a visit to my oldest sister, Adele, and her family. The wedding, however, went off wonderfully and Mary, my godchild, called to report that all is well.

There is no particular feast for this date that I am aware of. We will just have to rest content with my Dad's maxim to the effect that "Everyday is Christmas." He could always be counted on to say this the minute I got too excited about what I thought was the real Christmas, every December 25th. The older I get, the more I know he was right. Incidentally, in Cairo on the Feast of the Transportation of the Prophet to Heaven I was whisked to a tent where some fantastic, traditional dances were being performed[1] and in an effort to convey the significance of the feast, a galabia-clad parking attendant embraced me, thrust a sandwich of Egyptian cheese and bread in my hands, and wished me a "Merry Christmas"! I was so startled that I immediately took a bite, thereby breaking all my resolutions to watch my diet while on Cleopatra's home turf.[2] It turned out to be a great way to win friends and their trust.

Here's an excerpt from a poem that I haven't shown anyone, including David Bruce Duncan whose watercolor, "A Change in the Weather," occasioned its writing. Actually, David told me the watercolor was about my poetry so I thought it would be fun to write a poem somewhat relevant to a visual interpretation of the poetry (presumably) itself.

A Change in the Weather

is not all that difficult to observe
at first
but then
when it moves from warm to cool, and dry to moist
what evidence have we that
it is indeed the weather and not we
that has changed.
Why do we posit the flux outside ourselves projecting?
Surely we are nothing more than holographs hovering
surviving the holocaust in God's mind crucified.

If the weather never changes and only we . . .
then we have nothing to complain of or
delight in except ourselves . . .
and since we are always changing
then we are never changing . . .
and the reason for complaint or delight
evanesces and the Elysian Eliotian stillness,
a many colored rainbow, embraces the
eightfold path of Buddha.

Shades of Heraclitus! The relativity of our perspective on everyday reality will come up again in a later letter on science and religious education. For now, the holography reference is more immediately *ad rem*. One of my favorite ways of thinking about "what is" is to think of reality through a holographic metaphor. Holography has great arts implication. I'll elaborate on this in a bit. I promised above, however, that this letter would lead us to considerations of art in religious education on a practical level.

ARTS "REACH"

It is in the use of the arts to "reach" the learner that we arrive, at last, at a specific practical application in religious education. For I have found that the arts are one of the best paths to take if you want learners to meet their needs for transcendence. Thus, in a setting hardly operationally defined as religious, I have found that focusing discussion on the arts permits my students at the Board of Education, for example, to come more clearly to terms with their own transcendent capacities and their own reluctance to discuss them.

As you might well imagine, when I first introduce the Maslovian concepts relevant to transcendent needs in Eupsychian management, my would-be supervisors look at me in complete amazement, if not incredulity. And it is not without a considerable amount of effort that one is able to bring the concept front and center so that its applicability to work and the worker are clearly seen. Nevertheless, after the first onslaught of skepticism (if not polite disdain) an arts related discussion soon brings the seminar members to a feeling of confidence and openness about experiences which the surrounding bureaucratic culture would deem dismissable. Slowly, examples of transcendence through art-related experience (e.g., the ballet, the symphony, a Shakespeare play, etc.) surface and are shared. Gradually, the seminar members enhance their own self-respect, realizing that they have within themselves, each one of them, the ability to transcend the ego-beating environment and raise up their spirits above the dross of their daily hyperorganized operations. Moreover, as each member realizes that he or she is not alone in needing this kind of experience, the sharing of examples causes a flow of interaction that is indeed wonderful to behold.

Please note, Jim, that it is the arts that opened this door and allowed the students in a mundane, prosaic *management class* to deal effectively with their own needs for and their own experiences of transcendence. And while these learners were not seeking for religious enlightment, the same phenomenon, *mutatitis mutandis,* operates in the relgious education setting. I can elaborate on this point by recounting a recent experience with a young friend of mine who has been in trouble with the law.

As you know I have been working with small numbers of ex-offenders. One of the results of this work is a sense of great urgency. I may be overacting but my sense of the deep problems of our society has been greatly heightened by the last few months of efforts to help young people become a part of the "mainstream," so to speak, after they have been "out of it." Their name is legion. A recent trip to New York's Rikers Island facility (thanks to a student, Marion Hudson, who teaches on the Island) has left me almost speechless with the realization of the size of the problem. I am also speechless when I realize that the normal forms of motivation do not seem to operate with this population except in counterproductive ways. That is to say that money, glamor, sex, "action," etc. move them but, almost invariably, in ways that lead them back to the streets and back to Rikers Island or some upstate facility. I have never experienced such professional frustration.[3]

At this moment, a young ex-offender (you did not meet this one) has stopped by. He is either recovering from a night of gigoloing at a fashionable eastside disco or getting ready for another evening of the same. He just came in and asked me if I had any magazines. Guess what, I don't. Then he asked for "dirty magazines," and I remembered one of my former ex-offender associates had left a cache of his things here for safe-keeping in which I distinctly remember seeing a few of the racier magazines of our culture. I passed them along and all is quiet.

The request, and meeting it, may seem questionable to some but the least of my concerns in these cases is their affinity for pornography. Maybe I am wrong, but I won't discuss this further now.[4] I am, however, very concerned at the *use* toward which they have been taught to put their sexual natures. In most cases, it does not seem to be aimed in the direction of real and lasting self-actualization. If anything, it leads them back to the streets and back to prison.

But on the plus side—and this gets us into the practicality of arts and religious education—in this particular case (let's call him Paul), about a week ago, I took him, quite on the spur of the moment, to the Metropolitan Museum of Art. He's in his early 20s, has lived in New York all his life (except for the time in prison), and had never been to the Metropolitan Museum of Art! He actually thought that it was a place where art was sold. After getting the rules straight we went in. There, much to his amazement and to my delight he "grooved on" all the masters and the moderns. He began to speak of his own desire to be an artist. Now, you can hear a lot of things on the spur of the moment and so I thought no more of this visit except what I have already said. A few days later, he called me to tell me he had passed his driving test, gotten his job back with a fifty dollar raise, and was inquiring into art courses. All this and gigoloing, too?[5]

Let me hasten to point out that similar trips though the museum with similar individuals have not netted such a harvest. But, at least this case history reveals that with even the ex-offender segment of society, the power of arts to grab hold and inspire is very strong. In addition, the religious nature of much of the art in the museum led quite naturally to a confession of

Paul's desire to get his spiritual side back in order. We spent some time looking for renderings of his patron saint in the collection and piecing together sparsely his own religious history which, formally anyway, ended with a bit of church going ten years ago when he was twelve.

The foregoing is meant to be a practical example of a way to use the arts to help someone get back on the road to spiritual fulfillment. I realize that few religious education teachers will be in a situation to have the luxury of a one-to-one relationship such as I was gifted with in this example. Still, group trips to the local museum or art collection instead of regular Sunday class sessions would seem to me to a "natural" way to go.

And, as always, I am thinking first of the needs of the teacher. My own experience has been that if I meet my own needs in this regard then I stand a good chance of having others meet theirs. Thus, in the above instance, my suggestion on the spur of the moment was prompted as much by my own desire to go and experience the art there (I could live in a museum!) as well as by the hopes that the experience of my young friend might lead us along paths of conversation and spiritual/psychological work more productive than those associated with sex-selling, pornography, organized crime, etc. A group trip by a "class" to a museum as part of the religious education exercises would seem to me to be most desirable on the part of all involved.

HOLOGRAPHY

At this point I have to get somewhat provincial because of the presence of a special resource, the Museum of Holography, here in New York. As you know by now, my Platonic leanings find me thinking much of my life in terms of Plato's cave. In the Museum of Holography, there is perhaps one of the best arts-infused opportunities for religious educators. For, in holography there is a very dramatic graphic twentieth-century representation of the truths of Plato's cave so dramatically available that not to consider it at this point would be to miss one of the best resources available.

Curiously, I was thinking of saving a discussion of holography for the letters on science and religious education because the scientific implications of the phenomenon are equally dramatic. Indeed, I was first introduced to the museum by one of the most creative teachers I have ever met, Gerry Segal. Gerry utilized the museum as part of a new curriculum he developed called *Synergy*.[6] Synergy is a curriculum which fuses the arts, science, and mathematics in such a way that the students get a holistic grasp of the world of knowledge while enjoying it to the hilt. Thanks to Jerry, I have two of the first holographs ever created by New York City junior high school students. You might be interested to know that one of them is a holograph of a small plastic tray on which there is "sculpted" a representation of the Eucharist. It (i.e., the holograph) was created by a little girl in the synergy class who, for her holographic subject, chose this tray which she gave to her father on the occasion of her first communion. Thanks to one of those curious "synchronistic" experiences that make life really intriguing, I marvel that I investigated *Synergy* and its use of holography because of what I suspected could be its implications for religious education, only to discover that a little New York City girl had beat me to it. Her choice of holograph subject is perfect!

While I know from first-hand experience that you are very knowledgeable about art, Jim, I don't know how much you know about holography. I certainly am no expert in anything but the appreciation of it. You might be interested to know, however, that holography leans very heavily on laser technology (which the students are taught to use) and that an "acti-vated" holograph is a three-dimensional representation of its subject. The word "activated" is crucial here. For a holograph when presented in its unactivated state appears to be a flat surface, usually of a plastic glass- or film-like substance. What is not seen in this unactivated state is the fact that on this surface are thousands of tiny representations of the subject of the holograph. Thus, in the holograph done by the little girl the surface is that of a piece of rectangular dark glass. On the surface of this glass, unseen to the unaided eye, are a myriad of tiny reproductions of the tray itself. Once activated, (i.e., by shining a beam of light on it at the correct angle) the surface becomes three-dimensional, the viewer sees, in a very lifelike way, the tray which is the subject of the holograph. You can see why I went to investigate the phenomenon.

First of all, the thought occurs that art (and science) has come up with a dramatic demonstration of the fact that, to echo Saint Augustine, the whole of reality is wrapped up in one grain of sand. In this case, the whole holograph, so to speak, is contained in each one of the myriad of representa-tions that go to make it up. But even more significant is the fact that the holography is seen as a function of its lighting. What a great way to bring the truths of Plato's cave through to learners of any age. Just as in Plato's cave, the images on the wall exist only because of the ultimate reality of the light "in back of it all," so too the holograph gets its life and is seen as "real" only as a function of the real beam of light which activates it.

Let me repeat that I am aware of the fact that most religious education teachers at this time do not have a Museum of Ho-lography available to them. Nevertheless, I am sure that in the not too distant future holographic demonstrations will be uni-versally available. I hope you can see that this art form, both from the point of view of the "doing of the art itself" and from the point of view of the appreciative experience of the art itself (i.e., from the "consumer of art" point of view), is rife with potential to enhance the probability that the learner will come gradually to be aware of, and ultimately be able to habitually experience, the fact that things are not necessarily what they appear to be, and that in back of our everyday experiences lies a reality which can be experienced in such a way that our everyday perceptions appear to be illusory and life is better lived the more it is aimed in the direction of the knowable, "unseen" truth.

MOVIES

Getting back to the condition in which most of us find ourselves in religious education, I would like to point to two more art forms that would seem to me to be particularly appropriate for infusion into religious education: the movies and storytelling. In looking at these two art forms we are in a sense dealing with the newest art form and the oldest art form.

Considering movies as the newest art form means that even holography can be seen as part of the cinematic art since the creation of holographic movies should soon be commonplace. A trip to the movies (or the in-house showing of a movie) responds to young and old where they are "coming from." I remember when the Holy Humility of Mary nuns got us all into the Lyceum theater in Cleveland (now a porno house) to see a popular religious film at the time called *Keys to the Kingdom*. One scene with Gregory Peck may be appropriate to you and me when the reviews of this book come in. There's an unforgettable moment when he is hit in the face with an egg by one of his would-be converts. Oh well, *c'est toujours le même histoire*.

Curiously enough, with our permissive culture you would expect that there would be very few movies around of the caliber of *Keys to the Kingdom* that would be available to religious education teachers. But such is not the case. Two possibilities come immediately to mind, one rather recent, the other a bit older. As for the latter, it seems to me that Stanley Kubrick's *2001: Space Odyssey* is a good candidate for viewing by learners in the religious education situation. Indeed, as indicated above, the very title of this book comes from my own interpretation of the closing scene in 2001 when the wide-eyed embryo, placenta and all, fills the screen. It matters little whether or not my interpretation of the final scene is that of the writer or the director. For a work of art such as the film—like a word, according to Wittgenstein—gets its meaning from its use by those who would experience it. Moreover, the entire movie seems to me to speak to the "story of a soul" reaching for the transcendence which is involved with the destiny of all personkind.[7]

More recently, the story of *Close Encounters of the Third Kind* is a beautiful rendition of the "calling" given to men for transcendence. Indeed, the theophany scene at the end has occasioned in me one of the experiences that I have tried to describe to you as transcendent. Watching it on Cable TV in my apartment, I was gently pulled out of myself and removed to a place where I experienced being home, back where I came from, indeed in the lap of the universal father and mother. The experience was reminiscent of Bergman's finale to *Wild Strawberries* in which the professor envisions, idyllically, his childhood spent in the caring company of his parents on the banks of a beautiful river. (There, in Bergman, is a whole other storehouse of films, especially for adults, rife with the potential for bringing people to a good crack at experiencing transcendence. Indeed, Bergman, himself, has described his actual creative work as working with himself, his camera, and his God.)

Well, I hope that with this brief discussion of movies and religious education I can heighten interest in their potential for religious education in a front-and-center way. Practically speaking, I suppose, this means that some folks might band together to review movies for their religious education potential. Such a positive approach would seem to me to be a step in the right direction over and above the screening of them for their antimoral or antireligious postures—i.e., such as was done in our youth by the Legion of Decency. What would happen if movies were rated not on the basis of their potential to *undermine* the probability of transcendence but on the basis of their potential to *enhance* it? I'd certainly like to see something like that happen.

STORYTELLING

As far as storytelling goes, the universality and practicality of this most ancient of art forms cannot be neglected in any religious education curriculum that would hope to take advantage of the power of art. Everybody loves a good story and just about everybody loves to tell or hear a good story. Getting the little kids at the Uptown YMCA celebration of The Three Kings to tell the story of the three kings demonstrates the use of this time-revered art form in religious education.

As we at the YMCA plan for future celebrations of these three wandering Eastern sages, we are searching for constantly new and different ways to attract the attention of our YMCAers and bring them to a full comprehension, in so far as possible, of the mysteries of this feast. As far as infusing the experience with the arts, the story with all its miraculous and religious messages is beloved of artists for many centuries now. What are our options in arts-infused experiences? Well, to list just a few:

- −A presentation of the complete opera, *Amahl and the Night Visitors.*
- −*A scaled-down, puppet version of the opera.*
- −*A simple telling of the story with the kids playing the significant roles.*
- −*Doing a "shadow play" with the narration of the story, some simple background music, shadows cast with colored lights on a large white sheet stretched tautly in a space in front of the assemblage. As the story is told, the children, behind the sheet, will act it out in front of a light which throws their shadow images on the sheet for viewing by the assemblage. (Shades of Plato's cave.)*

These are just a few ideas. And, as commonplace as they seem, I hope that you can see the power of art to enhance religious instruction, leaning especially on the age-old art of storytelling.

ART AND THE PREHENSIVE CURRICULUM

I promised earlier to move our thinking about a prehensive curriculum along a bit further in this letter. How do these considerations of art fit in to this notion? To review a bit, the notion of a prehensive curriculum calls for various elements to be combined in the instructional mix until the desired effect is achieved. These elements in the mixture are added in until, so to speak, the critical mass is achieved and a uniquely new and effective curriculum "quantum" is achieved. The curricular whole, in other words, achieves a point where it is organically more than the sum of its parts and the combination of elements impact on the learner for increased effectiveness and efficiency in instruction.

I suggested earlier that among the elements of the *career* prehensive experience were a combination of Tyler's classic curriculum "filters" and three techniques of career/experiential education. Added into Tyler's three "screens" was the criterion of meeting the needs of the teacher. Thus, in the career prehensive curriculum, experiences are arranged for the student with components selected on the basis of:

a. teacher needs
b. subject matter requirements
c. learner needs
d. societal exigenencies
e. melding academic and vocational learnings
f. melding instruction and guidance
g. using the parents and the community as partners in instruction

The arrangement of experiences consists of selecting not only what will be taught but how it will be taught. In light of our discussion of art, above, to the above list of prehensive ingredients, we can now add

h. arts-related considerations

At this point I would like to make a departure, as near as I can tell, from the way treatments like this usually proceed. That is, I would like to make the point that what the notion of a prehensive curriculum suggests is not a step-by-step way of curriculum development nor a step-by-step way of teaching. Rather, what is intended in this presentation of the prehensive curriculum in religious education is a very flexible approach to a way to organize one's *thinking* about religious education as a *teacher* thinks about it.

I think that this is an important point. Over the years in my experience I have realized that teachers are much like I am. I don't mean to laud myself unduly in this regard, but what I am saying is that I steadfastly resist hard-and-fast, step-by-step, rigid approaches to curriculum and teaching. In saying this I feel that I am simply saying the teachers think in such a way that a highly rationalistic, positivistic approach to their "art" is for them, if not repulsive, at least highly dismissable. And, I think you will agree that all of the many so-called innovations over the years in education have left our classrooms basically the same in all too many ways.

On Sundays at church, for example, if I have occasion to see a Sunday School session or some such, I cannot help but think that the process I am watching in all its details is essentially the same process that occurred before the Tylers, Blooms, Getzels, etc. of this world came along with what I consider to be their helpful insights into the instructional situation. To me, the only reason that this is so is that the *mind* of the teacher has yet to be reached. Moreover, when efforts are made to reach the mind of the teacher, they seem ill-aimed. For teachers think intuitively, they chew on the matter they are pondering, they nurse things along on the basis of feeling; they do not systematically line up the ingredients of instruction and scientifically deliver them with precision. But maybe they are wrong?

I doubt it very much. I think that the way teachers think is perfectly all right. The problem is, the innovators in instruction have yet to come along who think the same way as teachers. If they did, they would never take the tack they do in presenting their analyses and results to teachers. To point out what I mean, let's consider again the notion of behavioral objectives.

Recently, in New York, I watched a disastrous introduction of the notion of performance or behavioral objectives across a good part of the system. My students, always fresh from the wars, are filled with stories of the debacle, and I wonder if the real greatness of Bloom's work will ever see the light of day. What happened? I am after all on record, both in this book and elsewhere, as espousing a performance-based approach to instruction. Why this fantastic rejection of a notion that seems really pregnant with great potential to assist teachers in enhancing their effectiveness?

I think what happened is akin to what happened when philosophers began studying the secondary qualities of sight and sound only to determine that what they set out to investigate didn't actually exist. That is to say that philosophers, when they decided to investigate sound for example, determined that there was no such thing but only matter in motion, impinging on more matter in motion. Similarly, educational investigators have studied the act of teaching and determined that its elements are really its totality, and armed with that erroneous assumption they have approached the teacher who, if lucky, escapes only bewildered, but all too often fails to escape and is crushed under the heavy hand of mandated instructions and procedures which are ignorant of the totality of the teaching act.[8]

Thus to reduce teaching to the movement along two or three continua of learning objectives (i.e., cognitive, affective, and psychomotor), or unduly emphasize this small element (e.g., by demanding very precise statements of objectives) of the teaching act is to be unable to see the forest for the trees.[9] Just as scientists have reduced all the wonders and beauty of sound to matter in motion, so, too, we in education often proceed as if we can reduce teaching to a simple or complex myriad of variables. No such reduction of the intuitive artist's act of teaching is possible. And so at this juncture I hasten to point out that in the career prehensive curriculum I am not suggesting a formula, recipe, or a protocol for curriculum development or teaching. Rather, taking a tip from some work in contemporary science which I'll address in a later letter, I am suggesting the career prehensive curriculum as a way of organizing, *not religious instruction,* but the *way we think about religious instruction.*[10] All I have to offer teachers in religious education is a way to think about what they are doing.

At first pass, this may not seem like an important distinction. But I think it is. I think that these considerations help us to understand teacher resistance to shaping behavioral objectives. I am not recommending that *all* of them *always* do so.[11] In this regard I think my position may satisfy critics like Silberman who survey the schools and see mindlessness,[12] and those who, seeing the mindlessness (or so they think), recommend super-tight, rigid, rationalistic systems of objectives and strategies and evaluations for all instruction. The position I am taking here says that teachers are not mindless; rather, they are intuitive. As intuitionists they can benefit from systematic insights into their behavior. As Socrates would point out, "The unexamined life is not worth living." What critics who accuse teachers of mindlessness fail to see and to appreciate is that the teacher state of mind is quite different from that of the systematic scientist. It is more that of the artist. And what critics who opt for systematic behaviorism in instruction fail to see is that what they offer teachers is all too often the equivalent of offering Michelangelo a paint-by-numbers kit. At best, it is seen as an insult; at worst, it is seen as destroying the very essence of the creative act of teaching.

Back now directly to what art brings to the career prehensive curriculum; How does art fit into this approach to *thinking about* religious education? Basically, and at the risk of denigrating it, it's just another something to think about. Probably most religious education teachers, when they do think about art will find that they have already intuitively integrated it into their instruction. Who has not heard the story of the primary-grade religion teacher who asked the children to draw a picture of God driving Adam and Eve out of the Garden of Eden only to receive back a wonderful visual interpretation of the Father at the wheel of a modern car playing chauffeur to the young couple in the back seat as they all head out the garden gate?

The prehensive curriculum asks for more than this. It asks the teacher to consider the arts, all the arts, in conjunction with the other considerations of the "mix." Thus, the considerations at this juncture in the argument include:

1. the needs of the teacher
2. the needs of the student
3. the requirements of the subject matter
4. the exigencies of society
5. the fusion of academic learning with the world of work
6. the melding of instruction and career guidance
7. the use of the family and community as instructional partners
8. the potential art experiences appropriate to the situation
9. the desired behaviors on the part of the learner

I, myself, find lists boring and I wish I could find a way to present this in a less didactic fashion. But I think we can rest in the consolation that it is at least flexible, for there is no intent to demand that every experience reflect all of the nine above considerations. Rather, the intent is to suggest to the teacher's nine "thoughts" (soon to be ten, when we get to science in the next letter) between and among which a teacher's mind can roam before, during, and after instruction, with the intended result that instructional decisions, intuitively made, will benefit from some of the best thinking about instruction I have run across.

It would not be fair of me to end this part of the discussion without some comment on the "looseness" of the above approach. In effect, all the approach offers is some *thoughts* on instruction. But that is all it offers because that is basically what teachers, especially experienced teachers want . . . and need. Teachers shape their own behavior, educationists don't . . . that much must seem clear. They also and necessarily shape their own thoughts on instruction. They must do this to meet their needs for self-esteem and ultimate autonomy and transcendence. To run counter to these needs is to invite more of the same, i.e., innovate debacles, teacher alienation, lower student achievement, etc.

I am also certain that many of my colleagues will cavil at the seeming laissez-faire attitude taken in the above discussion. But the laissez-faire elan which some might pick up is a relative phenomenon. If one thinks, as many of my colleagues in the social sciences still think, that the ideal paradigm of human behavior is the scientist in his laboratory being rational to the hilt, then the above approach will appear to border on chaos, if not irresponsible caprice. To them I can only promise to "justify the approach" by consideration in the next letter of the Heisenberg uncertainty principle as it functions (with all its implications) in modern physics. In short, the approach seeks to relate to teachers the way they are, not the way we would have them be, just as the uncertainty principle, by implication, addresses itself to the behavior of electrons around a nucleus (as we will see, a rather *indeterminate* affair) the way they actually behave rather than the orderly and systematic way we used to imagine they inhabited their orbits. And, if one would approach an electron for the purpose of making it a part of a bigger scheme of things (e.g., for the purpose of having it engage in a complex reaction) one had better approach that electron the way it is, not as one imagines or desires it to be.

Similarly, if one would approach a teacher for the purpose of having the teacher engage in a bigger scheme of instruction, one had better approach that teacher the way he or she is.

TEACHER EDUCATION

The last practical implication of the arts in religious education I'll mention rests in what all this might have to say to the preparation of religious education teachers. As I have indicated, I feel that only peakers can bring would-be peakers along. Thus, the responsibility exists for preparatory programs to enhance the future teachers' transcendental process. An arts-rich teacher-preparation curriculum would appear to be just the ticket.

We know that the arts are rich in transcendental-enhancing properties. We also know that teachers teach the way they are taught. If you argue for the use of arts in the religious education of students then you automatically opt for their intensive inclusion in teacher-preparation curricula.

Actually, at this point in our letters we can argue for what could be dubbed a "social-humanities"[13] approach to the preparation of teachers of religion. This curriculum would be rife with arts experiences laced with social-science insight. I wonder if we could not completely redo curricula and regular teacher-preparation curricula with this emphasis. Certainly better than a "methods" course in utilizing arts in religious instruction would be an arts experience itself developed over the years of preparation, replete with systematic understanding of it through psychology, sociology, social psychology, etc. For no matter what we seem to do with teachers, all too many of them still unconsciously imitate the experience they themselves had in college. Hence the omnipresent teacher-to-student, mostly one-way communication, the reluctance to use media (technical difficulties overcome), the reliance on rational, "banking" philosophies of instruction, and the tyranny of the normal curve. The thought occurs that perhaps such an arts-infused preparation curriculum for teachers of religion exists. I know of none for "regular" teachers.

CONCLUSION

Practically speaking, the arts in religious education can do the following:

1. Function as a most effective "reach" a teacher can make to the learner to bring the learner to openness to discuss and experience transcendence.
2. In their multimedia (including holographic and motion picture) formats, both in presentational format and in substance, familiarize the learner with transcendental motifs and experiences.
3. In a format as old as storytelling, elicit deep appreciations and new understandings of transcendental events.
4. Take their place in a prehensive curriculum for religious education.
5. Be melded into teacher-preparation curricula with great potential (along with social science insights) to create a religious education richly equipped to joust with the problems of enhancing learner transcendence.

I'll write the next letter in your honor on the Feast of Saint James which is coming up. It deals with science and the quest for transcendence on a theoretical level. The subsequent letter, a la previous letters, will attempt some practical implications. You probably have noticed that I introduced some scientific notions into my arts discussion. Indeed, if I am reading some of our physical science colleagues correctly, the hard-and-fast distinction between artist and scientist may not be all that hard and fast. If the tyranny of objective science is really over, what shall we make of the fact and does it in anyway impact on religious education as construed in these letters?

UNTIL THEN,
DAVID

Notes to Letter VII

1. The purity and blatant sexuality of the religiously inspired belly dancers were overwhelming. Such a powerfully erotic performance was the last thing I expected on this feast in the land where a blonde Caucasian girl in shorts occasions shock and reprehension on the part of the Islamic populace in a hot, noontime square in Cairo. The belly dancing was followed by an ancient stick-battle dance which combined athletics and art and, I think, religion, in as much as I detect a hint of transcendence enhancing in the pitched battle. The closeness of the warrior confronted with combat to achieving the mystical vision is a favorite religious theme and is perhaps best evidenced in the theophany in the Bhagavad-Gita. Arjuna is, after all, about to engage in battle when the Gita's "peak experience" occurs. I may be guilty of transferring a Hindu motif onto an Islamic phenomenon but in the context of the Feast of the Transportation it seems to fit. In any event, the potential of competitive athletics for transcendence, in a religious education program would seem to be worthy of serious exploration (as well as solo sports like jogging and skiing whose enthusiasts delight in revealing the remarkable "trip" effect of their leisure activities). While I don't include athletics in the considerations of these letters, they would seem to be another addition to the prehension designed to meet those with athletic needs. Perhaps this is a point for further study.

2. As you might well imagine, I had come to Cairo warned of intestinal difficulties inherent in eating certain foods because the Egyptians, seemingly not to their own detriment, fertilize with human excrement. Some microbe dastardly to the regularity of Westerners is present in certain foods and necessarily in foods already touched by Egyptian mouths such as this cheese sandwich. I hasten to point out that one can find bad food and water in New York, too, and I strongly urge a visit to Cairo no matter what.

3. A psychologist friend of mine who works for the city prison system responded to my frustration by pointing up the fact that I had simply come face to face with the criminal mind. When I queried him as to the appropriate "treatment" for such a mind, he shrugged his shoulders and said, perhaps a small number of ex-offenders living in close proximity (i.e., under the same roof) with a number of responsible adults for five years or so would stand a chance of normal societal success. This remark left me speechless at first, but as I have indicated to my students, these facts about ex-offenders, as well as the facts about our publicly institutionalized children (e.g., in the public schools) and the facts about the condition of the elderly—all these facts seem to argue for a new religious order (in terms of religion as used in these letters) made up, as I see it, of permanent and temporary members dedicating their lives to communal living with the needy (i.e., prisoners, elderly, etc.).

4. I'll try to tackle the sexual issue in a later letter. At this point I must confess that the discovery on my part of twelfth-century Tantric Hinduism helped me ensconce some current priorities in this regard within at least one strain of one of the world's great religions.

5. The predictable denouement of this episode consists of the fact that the job turned out to be in the "rackets," and the last I heard New York's Eastside is not bereft of a very popular purveyor of sexual delights for a fee. Nevertheless, the potential for arts to change behavior in a "total" program seems obvious to me. It would be a mistake, however, as has been done, to trust in the arts alone to work marvels.

6. Gerry Segal, *Synergy: An Interdisciplinary Mathematics Experience for the Middle School* (New York: Board of Education of the City of New York, 1979).

7. I referred above to a similar theme in *The Man Who Fell To Earth*. The fact that this film has become a "cult" film is interesting.

8. Thomas J. Sergiovanni and Robert J. Starratt, *Supervision: Human Perspectives,* 2nd Edition, (New York: McGraw-Hill Book Company, 1979). The thrust of this book, as I see it, is to point up the severe limitations of the overly rational and overly technical approach to teaching and learning. While the authors point up the inappropriateness of this approach to the *art* of teaching, the approach of these letters is that such an approach offends the *prehensiveness* of the teaching-learning situation, mistaking the part for the whole and falling into Whitehead's "Fallacy of Misplaced Concreteness" with a vengeance.

9. This passion for "precision" which haunts us in education today (in everybody's minds except the teachers') is worthy of note. In the letters on science and religious education I will point up that even the scientists, themselves, have gotten out of the trap of extending the precision of their own methods to the realities they study— thus, the principle of uncertainty, the principle of complementarity, and the theory of indeterminacy.

10. Thus, to many, quantum physics is not attempting to present us with the way the world is organized but the organized way we think about the world. As we will see, a universe of constant annihilation and creation of particles and antiparticles (matter and antimatter), with a curious habit of unpredictability by *principle,* certainly eludes being characterized as a giant clock a la Newton and Descartes which, once wound, follows determinedly through its motions. So, too, instruction, whose fluidity and indeterminacy is a joy, rather than a pain. True, the very nature of instruction can be appreciated by science, but without having the scientist project (or foist) his or her own passion for precision on what, in more ways than one though not completely, looks like the roll of dice. This thinking brings us to the question of whether or not God wound the clock or rolls the dice. More on this late-breaking story in the science/religion letters.

11. Alas, I have forgotten the name of a Westchester teacher who dramatically illustrated this point to me. Conscientiously, this elementary school teacher had worked with me and her colleagues on

the taxonomy. When, however, it came time for us to apply the taxonomy to an everyday occurrence, she chose to do so with her favorite lesson, teaching Haiku poetry to third graders. Well, her consternation matched mine and we both realized that one cannot capture an elephant with a net. Again, for all I know another teacher of Haiku may have taken to the taxonomy quite easily, but for me to have forced the issue in this case would have been ridiculous.

12. Charles Silberman, *Crisis in the Classroom; The Remaking of American Education* (New York: Random House, 1970).

13. Thomas J. Sergiovanni and Fred Carver, *The New School Executive: A Theory of Administration,* 2nd Edition (New York: Harper & Row), pp. 306–327. This book actually proposes a social humanities approach to *educational administration,* and the type of thinking the authors applied to administration is the type of thinking I would apply to prehensive teacher preparation. That's the way I am borrowing their term *social humanities.*

Letter VIII

DEAR JIM,

The summer is moving right along. The *New York Times* continues to be filled with interesting reports of youth in the drug culture seeking for the ultimate "high"; another story finds Norman Mailer's ex-offender protege wanted in a murder incident on the Eastside. It is difficult to work with ex-offenders only to see them revert to their ultimately self-destructive ways; a deep sense of disappointment, if not futility, must accompany such news for Mailer. As for the drugs, the release they offer youth is more a comment on what else is offered them than on the youth themselves. Raised as they are in a culture that affords them nary a chance of transcending the everyday grind, small wonder that they choose the path of least resistance and escape into their drug-induced euphoria. Both news items are equally depressing. I cannot help but wonder if what I have been saying in these letters has anything really meaningful to say to such problems. Sometimes I think it does . . . sometimes not.

I promised to write a letter or two to you on religious education and the physical and biological sciences. In doing so I am clearly moving (if I have not done so) into an area where I am out of my depth. Nevertheless, I make bold to put forth a few thoughts I have had in this regard in hopes of getting you to think through with me what the impact of the new physical sciences might be on religious education. I'll try to make this letter of a general nature, saving any practical specifics for the next letter, similar to the treatment given to the social sciences and the arts in the letters preceding this one.

To start, I doubt if the idea of writing these science/religion letters would have occurred to me if it had not been for a Sunday conversation with my friend and lawyer, Sal Viscardi, at his home on Long Island. Sal and I share a fascination with the workings of the scientific mind, especially in the realms of astronomy and physics. We have never allowed our mutual lack of background and training stand in the way of our explorations and observations in these two fascinating arenas. At best, we bring a fresh perspective; at worst, we "institutionalize" our pooled naivité.

In any event, on that Sunday Sal indicated that he was reading *The Cosmic Frontiers of General Relativity*[1] by William J. Kaufmann. What grabbed my attention immediately was his description of its contents as being similar to that of the *Baltimore Catechism*. I was intrigued, borrowed the book, and have yet to return it. And while I am not sure exactly why Sal said what he said, I have framed my own understandings of the book's contents in such a way that it can serve to speak meaningfully to religious education.

What books on the new astrophysics like *Frontiers* can do is open our minds to the existence of realities far beyond the sense data of our everyday experience. Indeed, the universe pictured in *Frontiers* and in other astrophysical treatises is laden with strange creatures like black holes, antimatter, quasars, etc. What is more, our own little universe seems but a speck in this mind-boggling configuration of universes.[2] As such, these treatises convey to the inquiring mind a firmer sense that there are realities as yet unseen, except in their effects, with which it remains for the human soul to come to grips.

If there is one underlying assumption of these thoughts to you, it is that the real stuff of "what is" lies hidden to us, unless through work and divine inspiration and grace we are brought to share in its grandeur. "Through a glass darkly," said Saint Paul. Since (as we have suggested) it is the task of the religious education teacher to enhance the probability that the learner will experience this ultimate reality beyond the here-and-now givens of sense data, then scientific studies like *Frontiers* can be most useful in alerting the learner to the fact that all is not what it appears to be, and that an openness to what actually are the *facts of the case* is called for.[3]

In suggesting that astronomy and physics be coupled with instruction in transcendence-enhancing religious education, I don't think I am suggesting anything all that new. As Thompson points out in *When Falling Bodies Take To Light,* to interpret an ancient myth without seeking to divulge its astronomical significance is to miss a good part of what the ancient religious myths were about.[4] Seen in this light, the ancient myths of religious experience are, from the earliest of times, imbued with a sense of the birth and structure of the universe. Astronomy and religion seem to have been linked for many moons before this one. To link them in these letters, then, is more predictable than not.

Indeed, even in the Christian scriptures, we find the study of the stars leading the three kings to the birthplace of the Christ. For these sages from the East, as "witnessed" by the evangelist, the wonders of astronomy pointed in the direction of the truth. There's somewhat of a feel for this type of consideration in the following excerpt from a poem of mine which, as is often the case, is an effort on my part to convey a religious experience. The excerpt is from a poem called *The Lovesong of Jay*

Alden Softrock: In the Morning. It's one of a trilogy I wrote, part of the impetus for which was to imitate, somewhat, Eliot's poetry. e.g., *Prufrock,* if not to do a gentle parody on it.

THE LOVESONG OF JAY ALDEN SOFTROCK: IN THE MORNING

Pange lingua. . . .
Introibo ad altare Dei. . . .
Suscipiat Dominus sacrificium. . . .

I

Let us stay then you and I
when the morning is spaced out against the rye
like two healthnuts energized albeit stable.

Out here on Spook Rock Road
the ravine slopes brambled gently
nettled
and the women threw it away.

The clouded meteorite. . .
pulsed cool yellow fire. . .
and its emblazened glory bathed us all

These my visions is all I have to give you.
The dead still living. . .
the emergent virgin. . .
the leaping from the cross King Christ
walking coolly through fiery wheat

As we look down upon us good and gentle Jesus
looking up while looking down at you
at peace beautifully on the cross
crucifixion turned to peace and glory
in blue space
while from our cross not contemplating

thy five wounds
floating up and out left standing
outside ourselves in the world ecstasy
of the crucified Christ, the end, the
beginning, and the central event
of all history is contemporary history
rising arms outspread the earth folding
twisting below and we above move now not falling not
running but passing into the dark
night of Christ's head black hole of the universe
through which the surprise is a light air
moving autoeidetic images take in a surrounding
enveloping, to which we rise, atomic eucharistic
procession and image surprise with the brightness of the
light while the hand gently kneads the unbaked, unboiled
raw egg beneath the water.

****

May, they will say
how his imagination is overactive!

Do I care? (Oh, have a peach!)
Why not reach?

Once in colonial silence I loved you
Could we go back further than that?

And in my loins at last
I saw the box
square black beclouded
within my entrails
auguring the smokey aftermath
of the destruction

painless as it was
no-waste land

And
oh yes
I think a poem is lovelier than a tree
especially one that's written by thee
necessarily of me
necessarily fasting

Out there on Warren Street
the leaking roof and buckled floor
must be balanced against
the energy escaping of Sadat and
the falling plaster too
near the place which will
last until the millenium
near the lawn where big-eared Buddha
with resilient sagging
tits
plays smiling grimacing with
da

d'Ave Maria
children and the snake
rising arms outspread the earth folding
twisting below and we above move now not falling not
running but passing into the dark
night of Christ's head black hole of the universe
through which the surprise is ah light air
moving autoeidetic images take in a surrounding
enveloping, to which we rise, atomic eucharistic
procession and image surprise with the brightness of the
light while the hand gently kneads the unbaked, unboiled
raw egg beneath the water.

I saw it all.
the nervous followers
the disco chairman and
levitating ecstasy

Before. . .
george the angel said
"I'll pay your way to the doctor twice"
then God the father then
God the son and now the
indwelling spirit constantly affording
merciful unrequited love. . .
the conductor wants no ticket and the drinks are
free on this luxury train to the
promised land. . . .
it's all free at last.
da
d'Ave Yahweh
at peace at last head resting serenely
sincerely in the left hand of the God-Man
da
d'Amen

The reference to the head of Christ as a blackhole through which one travels to emerge in a new light-filled Kingdom illustrates, I hope, the way the modern astrophysics can be used to bolster and enhance religious attitudes, postures, and experiences. Indeed, *Frontiers* and Sullivan's *Blackholes*[5] are two treatises which a layman can grasp, for the most part, and which seems to me to open the mind to unseen realities posited even in the physical sciences. Such "mind opening" can function as a propaedeutic to more profound realizations. Gradually our minds, immersed in the searing trade of materialistic commercialism, can be encouraged to rise above it all and seek for transcendent experiences of ultimate reality beyond the here and now, beyond even blackholes, quasars, etc.

I realize that perhaps not many people would agree with me that the effort involved in learning the new astrophysics is really worth it. And I suppose if the truth were known not too many Sunday School or CCD teachers have all that much interest in the so-called "hard" sciences and in their potential for boosting the effectiveness of learning religion. But I wonder if this is not a holdover from the brief but memorable reign of logical postivism. Am I wrong or are we still not too far from the day when the physical sciences were looked upon as the playground of materialistic atheism in which anything but the systematic, objective, and mechanistic treatment of data was inappropriate.

Perhaps I am projecting my own personal experience here, but it seems to me that I was raised believing in a distinct cleavage between the truths of faith and the truths of modern science. This cleavage is all the more curious to me in light of the fact that my own faith came to me rich in fifth-century B.C. science (i.e., *Aristotle* and *Plato* as brought to the West by Avicenna, etc.). In addition, I am aware of *Teilhard de Chardin's* opinion to the effect that science and religion would meld. Still, I have yet to experience a religious education program (granted my sample is small) that could be said to be imbued with the findings of modern science. And, while I anticipate great resistance to such a notion (I had a hard time getting myself to put this in writing), I think that the history of religious education, the history of the great religions, and the very nature of the new physical sciences make a more definite infusion of the sciences into religious education very desirable and appropriate.[6]

Regarding the nature of the new physical and biological sciences, a look at some relatively recent developments would seem to me to be particularly rewarding. At least two developments seem worthy of attention; the first, the Heisenberg uncertainty principle, once grasped would seem to me to break down some old antagonisms between science and religion; the second, the holonomic view of reality, has already excited Eastern religion specialists and will possibly come to greater prominence in more Western, Judaeo-Christian circles.

THE HEISENBERG PRINCIPLE

As far as the *Heisenberg* uncertainty principle goes, let me turn you over to one of my students from the most recent course I conducted at the New York City Board of Education. They say that your students will really end up teaching you if you really are going about teaching the right way. Well, in the case of *Daniel Fischetti,* I must have been doing something right.

We had been immersed in an introductory seminar on management theory, and I had, as usual, been emphasizing the importance of the Hawthorne Studies. Following is an excerpt from a mid-term examination in which Daniel managed to summarize beautifully the impact of the Hawthorne studies on management theory. Along the way, however, reflecting better than I could some comments we had made in seminar about the link between the Hawthorne studies and the Heisenberg principle, Daniel wrote as follows. He zeroes in on the "Hawthorne Effect":

The Hawthorne Effect refers to studies of worker productivity at a Western Electric plant in the Midwest. The effect of various lighting conditions on worker productivity were studied. It was found, according to expectations, that increasing lighting increased productivity. However, the experimenter expectations were dealt a blow when it was found that decreasing the lighting *also increased* productivity. Accepted theory had to be modified (or disregarded) to account for "subject effects"—that is, the effect of paying special attention to the subject. What eventuated was the concept that an observational study ends up studying someone being studied. This . . . brings us to the observation that the closer we try to study an effect, the greater the possible error—or indeterminacy, which is not quite the same thing. Thus, our better understanding of "subject effects" and indeterminacy has even extended itself into the realm of physical science where it is expressed in the "Heisenberg Principle," which simply stated contends that the closer the physical observation the greater the chance of error. This has been applied to the world of atomic and subatomic particles theory. The theory started with circular orbits, then moved to Modified Bohr ellipitical orbits, and now closer observation caused the need for the electron probability density cloud concept.

What Daniel Fischetti is alluding to here is the fact that the famous Hawthorne effect of the social sciences[7] seems to have a counterpart in the physical sciences in the Heisenberg principle. This effect in social science studies has been partially at the root of their being called "soft." This softness is, at least in part, the reason why educators seem to put little credence in the results of social experimentation. Whether or not you agree with me on this, I think you will agree that the Heisenberg principle brings more than a touch of "softness" to the so-called hard physical sciences. Indeed, according to the Heisenberg principle the closer you get in observation, the less sure you are of certain variables, even quantitative variables.

As a case in point, what used to be thought of as precise electron orbits about the atomic nucleus are now seen as electrons in a cloud around the nucleus with the observer having only probabilities as to the momentum and/or position of any particular electron. I think you will agree with me that this is certainly a curious "Cloud of Unknowing."

I think it was Bohr himself who indicated that anyone not shocked by quantum physics and the Heisenberg principle has failed to grasp their significance. Indeed, according to Popper what the principle does is knock mechanistic, deterministic, materialistic science on its ear and open the door for the fresh air of random, "freely occurring" events. It also brings to the physical sciences an air of subjectivity which heretofore would have been anthema . . . and certainly not all scientists are going to agree with this. Nevertheless, Popper goes so far as to say that the old "clock" notion of the deterministic scientific view of the universe must now give way to the "cloud notion."[8]

I think I am making two points here. First of all, the cleavage between hard and soft science seems to be more apparent than real. If nothing else, educators who downgrade the so-called soft sciences and their applicability and validity may take a second look at their reasons for doing so. Perhaps, after all, these so-called soft sciences are just as *hard* as the so-called *hard* sciences. Second, the path has been cleared scientifically for interpretations of the universe in undeterministic, holistic terms devoid of reductionism.

This last statement could use some clarification. If indeed, scientifically speaking things are not determined in a clock-work-like mechanistic way, then materialism is in trouble. Popper, for example, entitles his first chapter in a book with Eccles, *The Self and Its Brain*—"Materialism Transcends Itself." But what is beyond the material in science . . . to what has materialism transcended? The answer to this question is alluded to in a further passage from Fischetti's mid-term:

> The causes of all things begin to move into the realm of indeterminacy. The mechanistic science of the West begins to blend with the holistic philosophical and metaphysical science of the East. (All this from studying the effects of lighting on worker performance in the American Midwest?) Well, ultimately, it seems so. Maslow's peak experiences and Eupyschian concepts seem to approach the concept of "transcendental" experiences from a different angle, but these experiences do seem similar to the results of various forms of Eastern meditation.

The blend of Eastern religious thought and physics[9] is a topic which is surfacing at this time. It is a topic which also introduces the "world view" of holography as well as physics. While I dealt with holography in a previous letter on art, I also alluded to its scientific implications. The implication is that the holonomic model of the universe seems to encapsulate the conclusions of modern science and the tenets of mysticism.

HOLOGRAPHY

As far as holography and the new physics go, with reference to things religious, less than a year ago David Toolan did a very nice job linking these phenomena together. Toolan states that "as anyone familiar with recent physics knows, our everyday world of solid objects is built on a world of unsubstantial "blooming, buzzing confusion" where boundary and particularity, not interdiffusion, seem the miracle to be explained."[10]

If you think about this conclusion of modern physics, it soon becomes apparent that this world is mightily like that of theologies in which "we are all one." Thus the unity of reality seems to be surfacing as a truth of modern science . . . a truth according to which the "apartness" of things is more a mystery than their fundamental togetherness in the basic "one" of reality.[11]

According to Toolan, this finding, put together with Heisenberg's uncertainty principle, Bohr's theory of complementarity, Einstein's theory of general relativity, and findings regarding the nonlocal memory in the brain, has begun to enchant devotees of Eastern mysticism. Surely you can see that not only the seekers of the Atman experience would find these results of interest, but even a Western version a la Chardin's *center of centers* seems to find support in the scientific ruminations of these scientific pioneers.

There certainly is a Chardinian view of the world being approached or achieved here. The order of the world is *not only* that of things "lawfully" arranged and of events in a regularized series. Instead, each "unit" of reality has within its own intrinsic being the order of the whole "shebang" so to speak.[12]

Surely this discovery of the whole of reality in the part is a religious notion that we have known over the course of mankind's history. Now, however, it seems to be a scientific notion surfacing in observatories and laboratories across the world. Whether or not this is part of what Teilhard de Chardin spotted a while ago as the impending melding of religion and science, I really do not know. It certainly would appear that an interface between the two fields is of ever increasing interest.

Caveat: Determinism

What I have discussed above looks like a boost coming from the scientific community for some religious notions. While I admit there is cause for some optimism, there is also cause for some cautious concern. Moving now into the caveats which seem appropriate to the religious/science "coalescence," it's only a matter of balance to present a side of science which seems to move contrary to the directions indicated above.[13] I am alluding to the ever present and by now practically traditional materialistic evolutionism which is still very much with us. While scientists like Popper posit a creative evolutionism free of determinism and reductionism, the familiar mechanistic tenets of deterministic evolution are still with us. Thompson, in *When Falling Bodies Take to Light,* discusses this recurring scientific facet quite clearly in his analysis of sociobiology: "Fascinating as ethology can be, it does seem that its metaphysical generalization into the illusory synthesis of sociobiology suffers from Whitehead's "fallacy of misplaced concreteness." Selection, inclusive fitness, and the gene pool are concepts that become personified in sociobiological narratives, but at the same time that these disguised personifications are slipped into, true cultural and psychological configurations are reduced to physical genes that can be inherited."[14]

Indeed, scientific materialism is still very much with us, and E. O. Wilson, with his proffered sociobiological synthesis, is present to sober any who might think that the cleavage between religion and science is well on the way to extinction.

But even if there were not prominent scientific materialists in evidence today, a parsimony of enthusiasm would seem to me to best characterize any interface between religion and science. Sullivan, at the end of *Blackholes: The Edge of Space, The End of Time* says: "It is a special joy of scientific inquiry that no truth is absolute. No theory that attempts to describe nature can be complete."[15] Sullivan here seems to grasp the nature of scientific inquiry very well. Given the nature of scientific inquiry then, i.e., its relativity and its inherent incompleteness, it would seem to me to be mixing apples and oranges to expect a treatise on physics to systematically present the notion of the incarnate logos of a Vishnu or a Christ. Religion and science do have some aspects in common, not the least of which is that both, although in different senses, are pursuits of an ever receding horizon of truth. But the religious experience is not the scientific experience. Indeed, as I see the scientific experience in this century, it seems to be moving in the direction of increased relativity, with the scientific observer increasingly pondering the riddle of what exactly is being observed.

Is the scientist actually observing the configurations of matter in motion or is the scientist actually observing *the human mind* in the act of endlessly appearing to make observations with ever increasingly complex and sophisticated observational tools?[16] This experience is not the experience of transcendence. From one perspective, on the contrary, it is the experience of a mind trapped and folded in on itself. Religious experience, at least as I have tried to present it in these letters, is the experience of something *other,* something greater than oneself, something immediately "given" but something beyond analysis and understanding. In a sense, to understand it would be to destroy it.

Put plainly, I find myself increasingly leary of the so-called junctures appearing between religion and science. While I am enthused at the potential for science to "exercise" and "condition" the human understanding to be open to realities outside the ordinary give-and-take of sense experience. I still increasingly cavel at those who think that they find in the scientific discovery of the unity of nature the foundations (e.g., the Incarnate Word) of religion.

In other words, while I see the E. O. Wilson of our day erring on the side of reductionism, I look askance also at those who, on the other side of the issue, find the findings of science (and the tools thereof) sufficient to encompass the mysteries of religion. While I am not a Christian Scientist in any organized, normal use of the word, I find the following quote from the *Monitor* of July 2, 1979 to be of some import here: "The real universe is spiritual, created by God, and the law governing it is spiritual, not physical. Man himself is the spiritual expression of God. So-called physical laws are mortals' attempts to formulate what they see with the five senses. These laws are extensions of material mentality."[17]

Finally, my own personal transcendental experiences are of such a nature that I doubt if they will ever be reached through scientific observation.

This is not to say that the experiences themselves and my descriptions of them cannot be systematically looked at. In a way, one reason for sharing these experiences is to contribute to the data on such experiences. But the ultimate experience is not something you can see, hear, feel, or touch, although aspects of all these sense experiences can be alluded to. And even in those experiences where there is revealed a kingdom of transfigured matter, clearly the facade of the material universe we know is "peeled away" in the revelation of the glorified physical environment.

I seem to be at a loss for words here, and probably with some good reason. First of all, while I have experienced some Eastern-type contemplative moments, I have not experienced the granular *holonomic* details which seem to be the impetus to explore the unity of science and mysticism to some contemporaries. (The granular, photon-like aspects I *have* experienced.) Perhaps, therefore, I should say no more about this. But there are other Eastern experiences, like that of the yoginis experiencing the suckling Christ at their breasts, which certainly do not match up with any scientific findings. So perhaps I should content myself with observing that any congruence emerging so far between scientific discovery and Eastern metaphysics is partial at best.

But I guess what really worries me is the fact that we are dealing here with a two-edged sword. To rush to embrace the canons of modern science in support of mystical truths, while heartening to some, is to summon a gnat to bolster a behemoth. A reading of modern science today, especially in physics and astronomy, is certainly fascinating. But the last thing one comes away with is a sense of having experienced the ultimate. Rather, one comes away not only impressed by the conclusions but also chastened by the meagerness of our knowledge and the temporary nature of today's findings. While I can agree with Chardin that science can be inspired by mysticism and it can even lead to mysticism, I cannot imagine anyone's thinking that science *is* religion or that the laboratory and theoretical findings of science are one and the same as those of mystical experience. Science cannot remain science and be construed as transcendental.

CONCLUSION

In general, then, there is historical and current reason for religious educators to look to science to enhance their instruction. Certainly the scientific findings of the day have the potential to open minds to realities beyond the here and now of everyday sense experience. And while there is some reason to explore the congruence between scientific findings and models (like the holonomic model), the very nature of science and the nature of the transcendental religious experience caution us to ward off temptations to say that one is the other.

Writing this letter has been particularly difficult. I have left it several times to go consult the Hudson River to see what it has to say about all this. As usual I did not find out what the river said. That seems to belong more to my Eastern-oriented friends. Nor do I deny that it does say something, even though I have not experienced it as such. But I do raise an eyebrow at those who would say that scientific conclusions can say the same things. As you can't step into the same river twice, it is very difficult to step into the same scientific theory twice. The latter seems as flowing and changeable as the former. For this reason, and because my own experience fails to match these scientific considerations in detail, I suggest the study of science as enhancing religious education, not because of what is probably a temporary congruence between scientific discovery and a small part of the earth's mystical traditions, but because of science's capacity to open the mind to realities unseen, unheard in everyday experience. In these letters, then, science is construed as a propaedeutic and catalyst for achieving a mental and emotional posture open to the unseen and the as yet unknown. In this sense science can and has in the past led to mysticism. In this sense, then, science is most useful as an object of study in religious education programs aimed at enhancing the probability that learners will have peak, transcendental experiences of realities "beyond themselves." In the next letter I'll try to make some practical suggestions to religious educators who would like to incorporate science, so construed, in their curriculum.

I think I'll write you on the wedding day of Prince Charles and Lady Di. The Court of Saint James still lives. Until then, and . . . oh yes, happy feast day!

FONDEST REGARDS,
DAVID

P.S.   I'm working on a poem about all of this called "The Apperceptive Mass." It's been "growing" while I've been writing. I'll try to present it in excerpt form between the second letter on science (Letter IX) and the letter on some current issues (Letter X).

Notes to Letter VIII

1. William J. Kaufman III, *The Cosmic Frontiers of General Relativity* (Boston: Little, Brown and Company, 1977).

2. As we proceed through these letters on science, some rather technical themes will be introduced in the letters. Where I think it will be helpful to the reader with interest in more specifics, I'll put the specifics as I see them in the footnotes. In the case of the configuration of *universes* which emerges as a serious consideration in astrophysics and astronomy, some would view blackholes as entrances to other universes and quasars as the "otherside" of blackholes existing in other universes. Add to these considerations the "many universes" interpretation of quantum physics based on inferences about what happens to the collapsed parts of Schrödinger probability waves and you begin to see a picture of the universes which borders on—some would say coalesces—in detail with the Hindu view of the universe. As far as Christian tradition goes, Christ's "my Kingdom is not of this world" now can appear to be possibly interpreted in terms of this many-worlds, many-universes, scientific paradigm of reality.

3. I like the notion of "openness" as a prerequisite to transcendence. Indeed, as an ecumenical motif it seems to describe a characteristic of Hindu gurus, Christ, Buddha, etc. These letters, while espousing the view that religious education should enhance the probability that the learner will transcend, also espouse the view that this probability is enhanced by helping the learner to achieve "openness" to nonobvious realities. In these terms, then, religious education also has for its objective the acquisition of an openness to tran-

scendence. Thinking about it in these terms, the "probability" that we seek to achieve is operationalized as increased *openness of mind and heart*.

4. William Irwin Thompson, *The Time Falling Bodies Take to Light: Mythology, Sexuality, and the Origins of Culture* (New York: Saint Martin's Press, 1981), p. 173.

5. Walter Sullivan, *Blackholes: The Edge of Space, The End of Time* (New York: Warner Books, 1979). Sullivan is science editor for the *New York Times*. *Blackholes* is the type of popularization of modern science which is available to inquiring minds whose knowledge of mathematics, for example, is minimal or nonexistent. By the way, Einstein's own reputation for faltering achievement in mathematics should give all us nonmath types heart.

6. It helps to keep in mind that in a very real way science is the result of religion. The order that religion brings to many people's lives over the centuries, appears to be an impetus and occasion for mankind to seek order inherent in the universe itself . . . the quest of science. If one views the history of science this way, then one can see that we are in a sense turning the tables at this point in time, asking now whether science can foster religion, especially religion construed as transcendental experience.

7. I think it important to point out that recent "attacks" on the real validity of the Hawthorne studies leave intact the main "needs meeting" results and methodological results (i.e., the "effect"), at least as far as I see it now. I have not, however, dwelt on the aspect of exactly *which needs* must be met precisely. In this regard, Sergiovanni's position to the effect that "achievement" needs are the really crucial ones matches my experience. This position is laced throughout Thomas J. Sergiovanni and Robert J. Starratt, *Supervision: Human Perspectives,* 2nd Edition (New York: McGraw-Hill, 1979).

8. Karl R. Popper and John C. Eccles, *The Self and Its Brain* (New York: Springer International, 1977), pp. 3–35. This book, by the way, is not a popularization.

9. I am aware of the fact that I take a conservative view on this current and exciting exchange of ideas between mystics and physicists. At least it seems conservative to me. There certainly are times

that I can see and appreciate the *Incarnation of the Word* in terms of the new science. What I see is that the first "materialization," or in Plato's terms the first "emanation," from the nonvoid of potential is Christ, the Logos. Another case in point: David Bruce Duncan's "Holy Family" fascinates me because what a viewer sees is very much a function of the viewer. Some see the work as totally abstract and nonfigurative and do not see the Holy Family; others see a large penis to the left resting in an egg; still others see the three figures of the Holy Family. The "correlation" done of the givens in the collage is done variously by various observers. In many ways, then, what you get is what you see. Now, if one sees in the Holy Family an anthropomorhization of the Holy Trinity, then looking at the painting and seeing the Holy Family is seeing the universe and correlating the Trinity. All of this to me is interesting, exciting—good fodder for great meditation, but it is not as I see it good science. The leap of faith, though, required to correlate "to" the Trinity is certainly fostered and enhanced by scientific motifs. But science is not faith. (Notice, I may add, how the painting melds science, art, and religion in a wonderful amalgam with, to me, wonderful results.)

10. David Toolan, S. J., "Psychology's Theological Quantum Jump," *Commonweal* CVII, 18 (October 10, 1980), p. 565.

11. The mind, operating along the holograph model, correlates the bits of the ocean of potentiality thereby shaping the "boundaries" and in a sense giving birth to the thing itself. Yet even with the "boundaries" like the information in a holograph, every "bit" mirrors the totality, i.e., contains information about everything else. Pressing this phenomenon to its utmost implications, the door is opened for telepathy on a scientifically established basis and nonlocal causality in a situation where information can get around and be processed at possibly superluminal speed. If you think this sounds like lunacy, you are not the only one. Einstein never accepted these implications as final, claiming that God didn't work that way, in his opinion. Yet try as he might he never succeeded in disproving the facts and their interpretation along lines of telepathy and nonlocal causality. If you keep thinking along these lines, you can begin to see why the recent interpretations of quantum physics seriously chal-

lenge Cartesian epistemology, the objectivity of scientific observation, and the determinism of the "clock" model of the universe in which, the clock once wound, every subsequent motion thereof was determined.

12. Toolan, "Psychology's Quantum Jump," p. 565. Toolan relies on David Bohm's work at this point. The principle of complementarity is closely related to that of uncertainty. What it alludes to is the phenomenon that light sometimes appears to be a wave and sometimes a particle. Which is it—a wave or a particle? As I understand this principle, the answer to that question as to the exact nature of light is not available. Light is a particle if you set up an experiment assuming that it is a particle and light is a wave if you set up an experiment assuming that it is a wave. The nature of light is determined by the *observation* of light and, indeed, by the *observer.*

You can see why such thinking is appealing to mystics. Eastern mystics, for example, point to a unity beyond pleasure and pain. In the West, Meister Eckhart pointed to a fundamental "unity" behind the tripartite appearance of the deity as Father, Son, and Holy Spirit. Christ's line: "They are neither married nor unmarried in the kingdom of heaven" comes to mind as a mainstream example of such "complementarity" in religion.

In these letters, when I talk of uncertainty I am also by implication talking about indeterminacy and complementarity. Not only am I referring to an *in principle fact* of reality which means it (reality) is in itself significantly unknowable and unpredictable, but I am also alluding to the fact that even this indeterminate, unpredictable reality displays itself in complementary ways which define each other while excluding each other. Small wonder we are receiving word of physicists who are "walking off into the woods" like modern day Siddharthas, abandoning the preoccupations of the laboratory.

13. It is interesting to note that Einstein himself never accepted this interpretation and remained resolutely to the end a "clockwork mechanistic determinist." This fact, however, never impeded him in his own mystical appreciation of the deity. And a physicist like Heinz R. Pagels at Rockefeller University considers these philosophical/theological leaps to be gratuitous. This note, written in 1982, can

refer to his *The Cosmic Code: Quantum Physics As the Language of Nature* (New York: Simon and Shuster, 1982), pp. 181–182. For the "complementary view," or the other side of the coin, cf. Gary Zukav, *The Dancing Wu Li Masters: An Overview of the New Physics* (New York: Bantam New Age Books, 1980), and Fritjof Capra, *The Tao of Physics: An Exploration of the Parallels Between Modern Physics and Eastern Mysticism* (New York: Bantam New Age Books, 1980). This lack of agreement among physicists themselves, as well as Einstein's reluctance, help occasion the conservative stance of these letters regarding the religion-science interface.

14. Thompson, *The Time Falling Bodies Take to Light, pp. 55–56.*

15. Sullivan, *Blackholes,* p. 305.

16. When, for example, a viewer observes the painting "Holy Family" can it be said that the observer in effect creates that which he or she sees? Was the abstract pattern or the penis in the womb or the Holy Family there before the observer saw it? That's what I mean when I sometimes describe the painting as having "Wu Li" characteristics. Cf. Zukav, *Dancing Wu Li Masters,* pp. 28–9.

Incidentally, Zukav relies heavily on John Wheeler to explicate the quantum notion of the participator-created reality and Wheeler, reportedly, has recanted his "many worlds" interpretation of quantum physics. For this, cf. Pagels, *The Cosmic Code,* pp. 178–9.

17. *Christian Science Monitor* XXI, 52, "Skylab and Spiritual Law" (July 2, 1979), p. 21.

Letter IX

DEAR JIM,

Well, I seem to be hitting on some appropriate feast days. The last letter landed on yours and this one lands on Mother's. By the way, her portrait was delivered by the artist a week and a half ago. It was done by Whitfield Lovell, a young artist friend of mine. I will be interested in your reactions to it. It is not an ordinary portrait. Aside from its technical and aesthetic excellence, its portrayal of mother's personality is, at first, disarming. The portrait manages to catch her ever-present interest in life, her determination, and her unwillingness to accept the frailties of old age and impending death. All in all it is quite a success, although the first few days I lived with it were very difficult indeed. The eye of the artist brings many things home that selective perception over the years eliminates.

The writing of these letters is having a very strong effect on me. They have forced me to think through many of my own assumptions and, alas, I am finding my strong point is not consistency. What really bothers me is that my own perception of the inconsistencies is probably minimal compared to that which will be seen by the reader.

Not by way of excuse, but by way of clarification, I think I can say that as I write these letters, a phenomenon not unlike that of the Heisenberg uncertainty principle seems to be operating in my mind and feelings. What I am trying to say is that the more I seem to be investigating religious education from the transcendence-enhancing perspective, the less sure and determined I get about the best way to proceed. I keep grabbing for a synthesis of the ideas I have proffered thus far, and I find the more I grab the more elusive that synthesis becomes.[1]

I'll get back to this point a little later. For now, while the whole world is celebrating the wedding of Charles and Diana at Saint Paul's Cathedral in London, I'll try to focus what we have said about modern science on practical religious education concerns. To this end, this letter will deal with the relevance of modern science to a) the spiritual life of the religious education teacher, b) the use of scientific models and phenomena in instruction, and c) the integration of scientific themes into a prehensive curriculum for religious education. By the time I finish, the Prince and Princess of Wales will be on their honeymoon and I will have arrived at the juncture in this series of letters where I promised a look at several current issues in the religion/education interplay of the day, viewed in light of these considerations of transcendence and religious education.

THE TEACHER'S SPIRITUAL LIFE

As an introduction to addressing myself to the spiritual life of a religious education teacher, here is a poem I wrote some years ago. The poem "arrived" during one of my long periods of approach-avoidance conflicts with organized religion. I sometimes read this one (it's a favorite) and come away somewhat perplexed myself at what it is trying to say. In the main, however, it seems to reflect an attitude of mind and heart bereft of wisdom and solace from traditional figures, ready for the end of the world as we know it, and verging on some sort of naturistic religious future in which the trappings of organized religion are at a minimum and the world of nature reflects the peace of mankind's soul . . . both resting in the promise that God will never destroy the race. I'll try to explain why I am putting it here after you peruse it.

Thoughts on Entering a New Part of This Universe

It's really not a place . . . this dimension
where the objects of outworn beliefs are . . .
but are they, these gods and goddesses, ready
for this new crop, this motley crowd of bearded fishermen
not really accepting their fate yet. . .
the mystery of the once divine. . .
cool Minerva, fickle Cupid, how will you
relate to homespun Martha or uptight Paul?

I suppose if Jove has dwelt with Guatama
the Christ will rattle along from level to level
understanding and understood by this crowd
of bygone heroes

Maybe they'll all come back someday
maybe some new ones are on their way
this lack, this want now felt
is not incompleteness
faith is in the asking
. . . hurry back, hurry up. . .

And I'd still like to rattle around from level to level
there. This new crop of oldies
was different. Right, Zoroaster?

And Venus will peer at Mary and say
"I wonder what they ever saw in her!"

and back on the planet where the moon fell apart
part of it crashed, we knew, but where
we knew not . . . though with a bang
somewhat muted
and what remained was an ivory space ship
moving at hovering height over the
landscape until it disappeared

Bad storms came
On clearing we saw not a rainbow
but a sculpted-like rock terraced
inverted silently close earth staying and the
affirmation was once again clear and
closer to the fundamentals than ever
before . . . a simple presence

you feel like you'd like to but you're not supposed to
bow down. (Well, you can but only if you really want)

That's where I want to be with you
secure and airy rain-washed knowing
upon this rock, never denying
one . . . two . . . three
the rocky promise . . . no whiff of steam
refracting sunlight after a rain
into a rainbow but a
rock in light air hanging

I'm including this poem here for at least two reasons. First, it
reflects a state of mind inquiring into the truths and validity of
traditional wellsprings of faith. It is a state of mind which I think
must occur more than once in the spiritual development of
religious education teachers, somewhere along the line if not
perennially. Second, the astronomical setting of the poem and
its dealing with cataclysm reflects, I think, aspects of the scien-

tific milieu current today, which milieu might well serve to bolster the spiritual life of religious education teachers.

My concern for the spiritual development of teachers of religious instruction follows quite naturally from my concern for meeting the needs of teachers if they are to be effective and efficient. Certainly the spiritual needs of the teachers must be met—this is crucial—if they are to lead the learners along the path to spiritual fulfillment. And maybe I am projecting too much in this regard but I feel that teachers of religion in our antispirit culture can use every bit of enhancement they can get for their own steadfastness in their faith and their own growth therein.

Surrounded as they are today by adults and children who too often see and reject only the form of the particular religions, it is—or so it seems to me—very difficult to raise one's hands up, identify oneself as a peak experience advocate, and maintain this posture over time. I know in my own case that dealing with some of the rougher instances I have experienced has all too often found me with my back to the wall, unable to reach the learners in question, unable to counter their argument based as it is on their own experience of universal self-seeking and corruption, and in general questioning my own beliefs, values, and ultimately my own worth. With the little experience I have in this regard, I think it safe to say that one honestly gets more losers than winners, and one therefore needs every bit of support he or she can get in holding fast to faith, morals, and psychic (if not physical) energy.

It is for their utility as bolsterers of the spiritual life that I am recommending the reading of physics and astronomy as a practical suggestion to religious education teachers to enhance their own spiritual development, thereby providing them with the "stuff" they need to satisfy themselves and to satisfy their students. I guess that a few years ago this suggestion would have seemed somewhat strange. But we have had a while to digest the teaching of Teilhard de Chardin and Julian Huxley, and we have had the experience of the mysticism born of science which a Whitehead or an Einstein brings to our consideration. And while this mysticism-born-of science espouses, as near as I can tell, no one particular faith, it does seem to lead in the general direction of transcendence. But what specifically, you may ask, does it have to offer.

Reading the moderns in physics and astronomy seems to me to offer:

    a. A sense of how little we really know systematically and objectively about the world and the universe.

    b. A sense of trust in knowledge arrived at *sans* normal sense date.

    c. A sense of the magnitude of our surroundings (from astronomy) and a sense of the microcosms which surround us (physics).

It seems to me that a predictable reaction to the reading of books like Kaufman's *Frontiers*[2] or Sullivan's *Blackholes*[3] is a sense of how little we really know about the universe(s) around us and the matter at our feet. The humbling effect that this conclusion has is nothing but salubrious for one who would make the attainment of virtue the greatest goal in life. Humility, after all, is a sine-qua-non for effective human living. Conversely, however, what emerges clearer than ever is the certitude and validity of truths given by the world's religions and arrived at by religious, spiritual practices. Suddenly, on the landscape of what we know the two figures of science and religion look different—at least to me. The scientific truths suddenly seem, relatively speaking, hollow, fragile, changeable, even ephemeral . . . as opposed to the truths of religion which now appear to be stable, solid, reliable, and most worthy of lifelong commitment.

Thus, we appear to trust more and more in knowledge arrived at *sans* sense data than knowledge arrived at through the most systematic use of the scientific manipulation of variables . . . and broad-ranging theoretical extrapolation. Anything that can bring this truth of the *philsophia perrenis* home loud and clear to the workers in the religious education field would seem to me to be worthy of our colleagues' considerations. Once, for example, one grasped the subjective nature of the great cloud of unknowing of the scientist reporting conclusions on the great cloud of unknowing electrons around the nucleus, then the great cloud of unknowing which is a part of the spiritual life becomes, in perspective, a normal event in the pursuit of truth. And the doubts, fears, and ofttimes ensuing sense of futility which result from those periods when the whole world seems aimed in the wrong direction suddenly assume a normal predictable appearance even to the point of becoming a source of solace.

Lest the above sound to our scientific colleagues as if I am denigrating their efforts to the point of evanescent insignificance, it is also imperative to note that one of the constant truths of astronomy conveys the sense of magnitude of the situation in which mankind finds itself. At the same time, one of the constant truths of physics is the myriad of tiny microcosms which go to make up our physical environment. Echoing Teilhard de Chardin, this sense of "bigness" and the sense of "smallness" aid and abet our grasp of the cosmic significance of man's position in the grand scheme of reality. This sense, derived from the study of the physical and astronomical sciences, makes the truths of the world's religion all the more wondrous and all the more palatable, for they too focus on man and his "importance" in the scheme of thing. The sense derived from physics is of course not the sense derived from the spiritual life.

But even the sense of man's "centrality" derived from the physical sciences lays to rest objections of those who would fault religion for raising man to an unwarranted and suspiciously elevated position. The "wonder" of the *phenomenon of man* seems clearer and clearer the more our scientific colleagues pursue their wants. While it would seem (in my opinion) that their discoveries do not narrow the gap between the two modes of being—i.e., scientific and mystic—the case histories of mystic scientists indicate that theirs is a potent propaedeutic and/or catalyst available through the study of science—a propaedeutic to and a catalyst for enhanced effectiveness in making the leap to the life of faith and certainty.

Lest some of my religious friends at this point throw their hands up in the air at this recommendation . . . seeming as it does to want to make all of them scientists . . . let me hasten to add that there are sufficient popularizations available today which are quite able to convey to the nonprofessional scientist the "headset" that I am extolling. The Zukavs, Capras, Kaufmans, Sullivans, Asimovs, Sagans, etc. of the print and visual media are very handy and sufficient resources. Indeed, the creation of an annotated bibliography of such materials with a description of potential in this regard would seem to me to be a worthy venture.

Having, I hope, presented a reasonable enough case for the relevance of modern science for the spiritual life of the practicing religious educator, I would now like to move to considerations of the explicit use of scientific concepts, models, and findings in religious education.

SCIENTIFIC MOTIFS AND MODELS

In moving to considerations of the explicit use of scientific motifs in religious education, I am, in a manner similar to the treatment above of the social sciences and the arts, urging their inclusion in religious education curricula in an "up front" way. Just as Aquinas found the science of the ancient Greeks useful to his presentation of systematic theology, so too, I am arguing that "new Aquinases" might look seriously to the explicit use of contemporary science in explicating the truths of religion.

In the letters on the arts I said that I would consider the implications of holography (and the holonomic model of reality) under the umbrella of the arts—although I noted at that time that it would be equally at home under the scientific category. I'll rest with that decision with the further note that this intriguing conjuncture of science and faith certainly seems worthy of much more explication.

And indeed it certainly seems to be getting coverage. For example, the latest issue of Revision,[4] from an ashram in Cambridge, seems to be evidence of a growing fascination. I would like to join in the search, but perhaps that is a topic for a future series of communications between us. At the same time I think that Hobbes observations about science and religion need to be aired at this time. As I recall he indicated that the last thing to be sought would be the making of the experience of God an experience within the confines of scientific inquiry. I think the thought is still valid. And here, at least at this point in time, I draw back from those who look forward to future physical science treatises on the nature of the universe handling within the parameters of physics the incarnation of the word. Science can open our minds to the possibilities of religious truths, it can exercise our minds to a point of readiness for grasping truths of the mysterious, but it cannot, as I see it, encapsulate in its rational modes the ineffability of the transcendent.

Moreover, the danger of a bandwagon in this regard seems clear. The changeability of scientific fashion is a matter of public record. On this basis alone it would be precipitous and counterproductive to both religion and science to cement their merger; counterproductive to religion, for the predictable emergence of new scientific theories would render any marriage with "old" theory invalid; counterproductive to science because of the tendency such a religion-science wedding would have to fix in concrete and render immutable scientific truths which are by their nature working hypotheses and, perhaps, at their most "truthful" and useful, when they begin to show signs of age, unfashionableness, and imminent collapse within the scientific arena.

Magnetism

With these reservations as to what I am about, then, I would like to consider the usefulness of the explicit use of scientific models in religious education. The best way to do this, it seems to me, is to explain what I mean through some examples. I hope by proceeding in this way to demonstrate that the use of science in religious education is not to be reserved only for those who have the increased sophistication that is too often attributed to those who think scientifically. I also hope to demonstrate that it is not all that difficult to bring scientific motifs to bear on day-to-day religious instruction.

For my examples I choose motifs of magnetism and evolution, two scientific developments not too far away from the everyday mental state of the common individual. I have used both motifs in situations where I have been making every effort to bring management students to the realization that they are "surrounded" by entities beyond sense data which nevertheless are capable of being experienced. At least, using the motifs of science, I have a chance to point out to them that the existence of such entities does not offend the best scientific sense even if it does seem to run contrary to their own common sense.

Again, I am reminded of my basic unworthiness to be writing these letters to you. Still, I will press on, reminding you of my earlier resolve to bring my experience in public and secular education to bear on religious instruction. The link between the two educational worlds (i.e., religious and secular) in my own experience becomes evident when motifs of unseen entities and transcendent experiences surface. As I indicated above, these transcendent motifs are common to both worlds, and, for me, they form the bridge between the two domains.

Thus, for example, in teaching management I find myself faced with conveying to a class what Chester Barnard means when he says that an organization does not consist of individuals, is not comprised of the "group," and does not exist primarily in space.[5] These notions do not set easily with many of my students who have difficulty envisioning exactly what Barnard is trying to get at. Luckily, Barnard himself has at his disposal a scientific motif to help convey his meaning. He uses magnetism to help move his readers minds to an appreciation of the existence of an "entity" which in effect is unseen and unheard and is something which exists over and above the existence of the individuals and the groups which go to make it up. He asks us to consider a magnetic field.[6]

Note, he points out, how the spatial parameters of a magnetic field can not be determined. Indeed, any magnetic field is theoretically *infinite*. Moreover, it cannot be seen—only its effects can be seen. Thus, the magnetic field of a "group" of magnetic filings is not the filings themselves, nor is it the group of filings. Rather, the fact that a field exists at all is determined from its effects on the filings, and it would be a gross mistake to think that which is effected is that which is doing the effecting.

I have watched for almost ten years now how the earlier skepticism of my students dissipates with the use of this scientific model. Their earlier negative reactions to understanding an organization as an invisible force quite apart from its "members" gives way to a sense of wonder with a lingering patina of consternation. This is a thought that is quite fresh and brand new. The power of the magnetism model is that it opens their eyes to the significant possibility that, in organized life, there is a separate force operating that is quite unseen and unheard and which is nevertheless immensely powerful—indeed, powerful over and above the efforts of individuals or grouped individuals formerly conceived of as a part of the organization.

Such thinking on the part of my students leads me to think that this magnetic model could be used to good effect with all ages in religious instruction. As a matter of fact I have on my desk a simple apparatus given to me by John Kominsky, one of my students. John is assistant director in the Office of Science Education at the Board of Education of the City of New York. When we considered Barnard's hypothesis and its meaning, John took immediate interest in the use of the magnetic model and brought in to me the apparatus. It consists of a glass vial filled with mineral water in which there are magnetic filings. To complete the equipment, there is a powerful horseshoe magnet. Now, when I get to this part of Barnard, I can simply pass this apparatus around and let the mind "take off" from there. There *are* forces which are invisible and which are theoretically infinite.

What I am suggesting is that this simple magnetic model can be used to good effect in any situation designed to bring students minds to a readiness to grasp realities beyond the ken of everyday sense experience.

For example, while writing this I have just made a slight rearrangement of the magnetic apparatus John gave me and the sheer wonder of it all is still fresh. Isn't such a demonstration of "power" applicable to religious education, at least as conceived in these letters? When I turned the vial, leaving the magnet in approximately the same position, the filings began to follow it. I have just taken another look . . . and wonder of wonders, the filings have formed a "mirror image" of their own in the glycerin . . . a mirror image, that is, of the horse-shoe magnet. It looks sort of like a rainbow of metal bits hanging in the mineral oil. You see (and I didn't know this until now), the apparatus can be used not only to point to unseen forces over and above individual human beings, but forces which have the effect of replicating themselves in some form or other in our lives. I have to confess, I had no idea that a magnet would do this. Thank you, John! The filings have simply arranged themselves in a form as close to that of the horse-shoe magnet as they could. Or, better, the magnet has brought the filings into a shape as close to the form of a horseshoe as they or it could achieve. "In the image and likeness," "We are Atman" . . . how this simple science demonstration speaks to unseen, unheard forces shaping our lives in ways germane to the teachings of the worlds' religions. I must say, I am loathe to move the apparatus on my desk. It is too good to be true.

Evolution

Another model from science that I frequently use under similar conditions is that of evolution. I suppose that before I go into a discussion of evolution that I should point out my own reservations about evolutionary theory. Richard and Martha Chiriani gave me a copy of Richard Leakey's *Origins*[7] for Christmas in 1979. I read it soon after and quickly developed a reaction that surprised me. The reaction was one of increasing skepticism, perhaps not unlike that of Mark Twain who "delighted" in the wholesale conjecture that such a minimal fact can generate in science. I remember being particularly disturbed by my reaction, especially because I knew that Richard and Martha (who I assumed would be evolutionists) would be looking forward to hearing it. Finally, I just confessed to them one evening, in the midst of a long conversation, that the theory seemed to be a large edifice built on shaky ground. Much to my surprise and delight, both Richard and Martha looked at me approvingly and accepted my skepticism as a "right on" reaction. Thus, when I do use evolutionary theory in instructional episodes I do so realizing that, for all its wonders, it is only science which is necessarily subject to change at any time.

Nevertheless, out of the scientific study of the "evolution" of man have come some interesting motifs which are highly conducive to alterting minds to the existence of realities beyond sense experience. The evolutionary considerations I would like to bring to bear at this point have to do with the dimensions of reality (or evolutionary plateaus) which are common to many thinkers in evolutionary circles. A good example of what I mean is included in the following "lineup" from Karl R. Popper:

World 3 (The products of the human mind)	(6) Works of Art and of Science (including Technology) (5) Human Language—Theories of Self and of Death
World 2 (The world of subjective experiences)	(4) Consciousness of Self and Death (3) Sentience (Animal Consciousness)
World 1 (The world of physical objects)	(2) Living Organisms (1) The Heavier Elements: Liquids and Crystals (0) Hydrogen and Helium

FIGURE 2.   POPPER'S TABLE OF SOME COSMIC EVOLUTIONARY STAGES[8]

Popper's "three worlds" delineate for him "some Cosmic Evolutionary Stages," and this kind of thinking seems common to many "evolutionists." That Teilhard de Chardin's thinking is still seen in such thinking attests to the longevity not only of this evolutionary theory but also to the keenness of his own thinking along these lines.[9] As one proceeds "up" Popper's evolutionary stages, it is easy to "lay over" the Chardinian observation that the complexity of being increases as one goes up the evolutionary ladder; as the complexity of reality increases, i.e., from 0 to 1 to 2 in Popper's World 1 or, more broadly from World 1 to World 2, the emergence of consciousness becomes apparent. Thus, there is a correlation between complexity and consciousness such that one can observe that the more complex a reality, the more consciousness can be attributed to it.

I have found such scientific motifs to be a great help in bringing my students to accepting the fact that it is possible that there are conscious entities beyond their sense experience which nevertheless they can experience. Such an entity is, at least as I interpret it, Barnard's *organization*. Barnard considers an organization to be a social creature, "alive."

When my students first meet this concept, they meet it either with skepticism or with a tendency to water Barnard's thought down to the point where his use of the word "alive" is an analogical use at best.[10] But in order to get them to see the possibility that he could be quite literally interpreted as intending organization to be seen as a *conscious being* with, so to speak, a mind and will of its own, I use evolutionary thinking to show them that science itself can be content with such a notion.

If complexity, so to speak, "breeds" consciousness and supercomplexity, such as in the human brain, "breeds *self*-consciousness," then an organization, itself a complex of very complex consciousnesses in an intricate complex configuration, can be seen along the evolutionary developmental line as a new "superconsciousness," existing over and above the individual consciousnesses contributing to it.

Thus, I urge that to Barnard an organization is like a magnetic field inasmuch as it is not seen or heard but yet is very forceful. Moreover, it does not exist primarily in space, and it does not consist of its individual members. To be more exact there are not members of an organization but only contributors to the organization. Certainly the contributions, as the filings in a magnetic field, are not the field or the magnet, are not the organization. And, moreover, whatever this strange entity is we call *organization,* it has consciousness of its own, i.e., it has, so to speak, a mind and will all its own with its own view of reality and its own priorities over and above those of the individual contributors.

Now, it seems to me that what is important here is not that you necessarily agree with the conclusions this type of thinking leads you to. What is important is that you see that this type of thinking renders more plausible a hypothesis to the effect that in organized life an individual is faced with an invisible consciousness over and above his own or anybody else's "in" that organization. Even if the conclusion still sounds strange, I hope you can see that it is not without its precedence and foundation even in scientific thought.

This evolutionary motif seems to me to have significant potential for us in religious education, as it is construed in these letters. For this type of thinking opens the mind to the distinct possibility that conscious beings exist which we cannot directly see, hear, taste, etc. Once more, scientific motifs have led us to the threshold of doors which, if opened through faith and work, can afford the soul the immediate grasp of a something greater than self with which one can commune. The insight such reasoning gives to Christ's "wherever two or more of you are gathered in my name, there also I am" is, at least, impressive.

The use of science in experiences designed to bring students to a better chance at achieving "transcendence" would seem to me to be perfectly reasonable. I hope you agree. Based on evolution, belief in superconscious beings with a potential for transcendental union by the individual appears within the purview of scientific understanding.[11]

THE PREHENSIVE CURRICULUM

The final aspect of this topic I would like to treat in this letter is the inclusion of scientific motifs in the prehensive curriculum I have suggested before for religious education. Simply construed, this foregoing discussion means that to the list of prehensive elements we add scientific motifs. And perhaps rightfully so; the heart of dedicated and sincere religious education teachers may be fainting at the notion that this list seems never ending.[12]

Well, the addition of the scientific elements to the list yields the following considerations as germane to a prehensive curriculum in religious instruction:

1. The needs of the teacher.
2. The needs of the student.
3. The requirements of the subject matter.
4. The exigencies of society.
5. The fusion of academic learning with the world of work.
6. The melding of instruction and career guidance.
7. The use of the family and community as instructional partners.

8. The potential art experiences appropriate to the situation.
9. The potential science experiences appropriate to the situation.
10. The desired behaviors on the part of the learner.

As I said above, I am not that much enamored of lists. And I certainly would like to line these "elements" up in a more systematic fashion. But the fact of the matter is the more I try to line them up systematically, the less they seem capable of such a systematic lineup. In effect, if you think through this list of elements you will invariably arrive at a sense of frustration at their "indeterminacy." In other words, like electrons in the atomic cloud, the more we try to understand the precise position of each of these components in the "hierarchy" of prehensive instruction, the less likely it appears that we will even be able to lock even one of them in. This indeterminacy which some may find disturbing is nevertheless echoed in science itself in Heisenberg's uncertainty principle implying as it does indeterminacy.

But this list is only highly indeterminate in its order of priority. Indeed, under consideration each element seems to be included in every other element. What reaction shall we make to the fact that after all these pages we are faced with a curricular lineup composed of collapsing concepts hardly distinguishable one from the other under casual scrutiny? Can we rest content, for example, with the fact that prehensive consideration number one—i.e., the needs of the teachers—when really thought through includes every other consideration. That is to say, the needs of the teacher embody societal requirements, don't they? And societal requirements certainly embody the world of work and all its exigencies . . . and scientists and artists are a part of the world of work aren't they? So number one in effect contains all ten.

But rather than frustration at this experience of the many in the one, we perhaps can take some satisfaction. For what we have discovered in the realm of religious, prehensive, education is a rather holonomic world in which the whole seems to be reflected in each part. In light of what we have said above, I hope you will agree we are in some interesting company.

Such a world this study of education leaves us! But we can take heart! With the advent of the quantum physics, the holonomic model of the universe, etc. the tyranny of objective, hard science is over, and at least we don't have to be ashamed at our own uncertainty and the indeterminacy of elemental configuration and conceptual precision. Rather, we can take some comfort from the fact that we have simply arrived at a rather awesome truth, viz, that ultimately reality is one, and in knowing it, the more we know, the more we know there is more to know.

Moreover, while I said I didn't like lists, I think I should qualify that remark. What I meant was I don't like lists when I am trying to be scientific and systematic. But teachers like lists. Give them a list of materials, or a list of books in a bibliography, or a list of resources, or even a list of objectives and strategies and they can be quite content. They are aware of the fact that they will set their own priorities no matter what the administration says. In addition they will pick and choose from any list you might give them. Their autonomy as teachers permits them this picking and choosing. Take this autonomy away from them and they, as they are doing now in our large stressful bureaucratic school systems, burn out. Take this autonomy away and you take away their self-respect.

And so the last thought in this religion-science letter is about the autonomy and self-respect of teachers. We end, then, not with a bang or a whimper, but with a call to teachers to look at our list, to pick and choose from it if it is helpful, and to sustain thereby their own sense of fitness, dignity, and spiritual well-being. Unless this is achieved and they experience autonomy in the instructional situation, they will be hindered from achieving their greatest need . . . the need to transcend self and experience loss of self without destruction of self in union with something greater than they.

Well, the Prince and Princess of Wales are honeymooning, the baseball strike is ending, and I am nearing the end of this series of letters to you. Only two more to go. You ought to know that these last two letters on science were really a challenge to write. I found myself moving into areas of considerations that I didn't envision before I began to write. The validity of what I have to say remains to be seen. I am pleased to report, however, that a young friend of mine, John McCormick, stopped by as I was writing this letter to touch base with me before he took off for permanent residence in an ashram in Cambridge affiliated with Swami Chetanananda.[13] I was able to share some of these considerations of science and the spiritual life with John, and we seemed to come to the conclusion that I had somehow or other managed to arrive at some reasonable conclusions . . . for now, anyway.

And . . . for now . . . farewell. I am not sure when I will write the last two letters. Fr. Paul Byrnes is coming in on the 19th and I will be taking off for Deep Creek Lake on August 20 to spend some time in the mountains. Maybe that would be a good place to tackle the last letter. Until the next time

INDETERMINATELY YOURS,
DAVID

P.S. The science/religion poem follows before the next letter.

Notes to Letter IX

1. The impact of the Heisenberg uncertainty principle cannot be underestimated. Because I rely on it in these letters so heavily now, I think it important to point out that it is a *principle* limiting our knowledge of the world, not because our knowing powers are limited, or because we await better technology to help us see better. Rather, what Heisenberg and others have demonstrated, and according to some without a doubt, is that the universe in and of itself is indeterminate, making our knowledge indeterminate.

You will recall I was dating a math major while I was at Notre Dame and thanks to her I discovered that math majors were leaving the math stalls in droves because they had determined that truth was not available through that route, i.e., math. I thought that was curious since I, unlike they, apparently had never subscribed to the notion that somewhere, available to man's capable mind, was the *one formula* that explained everything. Maybe they were leaving because someone had plumbed Heisenberg's depth and realized that what quantum physics says is that, *by principle,* there is no such formula. In fact and effect, God plays dice. Even God doesn't know the future in all its detail. God not only likes but is full of surprises.

Here are some references that will help anyone who wants to look at this in detail. I must say it's a slippery notion but worth the effort to explore. And it does permit one to discuss at cocktail parties the "double-slit experiment" in which photons process information consciously at superluminal speed. The upper Eastside hasn't been the same since: 1) Gary Zukav, *The Dancing Wu Li Masters: An Overview of the New Physics* (New York: Bantam New Age Books, 1980), pp. 27, 35, 111–114, 209, 223, 230, 235, 241, 246, 308; 2) Fritjof Capra, *The Tao of Physics, An Exploration of the Parallels Between Modern Physics and Eastern Mysticism* (New York: Bantam New Age Books, 1980), pp. 136–145; 3) Heinz R. Pagels, *The Cosmic Code: Quantum Physics As The Language of Nature* (New York: Simon and Schuster, 1982), pp. 87–91, 93, 96–97, 163–164, 275–77.

Related to the Heisenberg principle is the complementarity principle which "sort of" operates when you look at the "Holy Family" collage. You can't see both the figures and a nonfigurative abstract at the same time. Yet both are real aspects of the same underlying reality. Thus, in subatomic particle experiments sometimes light is observed as a photon and sometimes as a wave. But *what is light?* Well, it's something that appears as a photon sometimes and sometimes as a wave. There is an underlying reality *not directly observable by us,* indeed, even in what we observe, i.e., a photon; if I want to know its position then I can't precisely determine its *momentum,* and if I want to measure its *momentum* then I can't precisely determine its *position.*

Heisenberg's uncertainty principle, Born's indeterminacy theory, and Bohr's complementarity principle, together in all their relatedness, make up the basic building blocks of quantum theory. Heisenberg's work actually implies the tenets of indeterminacy. When it comes down to *what is real* in quantum physics (at least in the interpretation of many physicists) you get to the level of observing the same thing as complementary appearances. And even as regards what you observe, which cannot be the *basic* reality, you are limited about what you can determine *in principle.* The slipperiness of all this had led to theories of observer-created reality. For example, if you see a penis in the collage, it is *you* who are "correlating" the information to see the penis; if you see the Holy Family, it is *you* who are correlating the information to see the Holy Family. Ultimately, you can ask the question who is correlating what so that you yourself appear? God? It's fascinating. But, down to business. Here, for those interested, are some references on complementarity from the same three books: Zukav, *The Dancing Wu Li Masters,* pp. 93–95; Capra, *The Tao pf Physics,* p. 145; Pagels, *The Cosmic Code,* pp. 86–87, 91–96, 103, 188.

2. William J. Kaufman III, *The Cosmic Frontiers of General Relativity* (Boston: Little, Brown and Company, 1977).

3. Walter Sullivan, *Blackholes: The Edge of Space, The End of Time,* (New York: Warner Books, 1979).

4. *Revision: A Journal of Consciousness and Change* IV, 1 (Spring, 1981). In this issue a section called "Forum: Science and Mysticism," pp. 22–86, illustrates some current coverage.

5. Chester I. Barnard, *The Functions of the Executive* (Cambridge: Harvard University Press, 1938), pp. 68, 81.

6. Ibid., pp. 75–76, n.

7. Richard E. Leakey and Roger Lewin, *Origins* (New York: E. P. Dutton, 1979).

8. Karl R. Popper and John C. Eccles, *The Self and Its Brain* (New York: Springer International, 1977).

9. Teilhard de Chardin, *The Phenomenon of Man* (New York: Harper Colophon Books, 1975). I realize that much of my thought has been influenced by Teilhard de Chardin, and in a sense I take much of his thinking, in overall matters, for granted now. It is interesting to note that I first was seriously introduced to him and *The Phenomenon* after my LSD experience, which incidentally took place "around the corner" from the Stanford Accelerator which figures so prominently in quantum and subatomic particle physics. I was not too happy with what had happened for a lot of reasons, but my "gurus" advised me to begin to integrate what had happened to me over time. To assist in this integration, they suggested that Teilhard had said, in one way anyway, what I had experienced under the drug. I can't resist, also, wondering at the proximity of the LSD administration site and the Stanford Accelerator. God works in strange ways. I wonder if this was one of them.

10. Barnard, *The Functions of the Executive,* p. 259. On this page Barnard clearly speaks of the "living system of human efforts" which is the organization and at this point I have little doubt but that he meant just that, *alive.*

11. In effect, what we have in Barnard's living conscious organization is another scientific basis for mysticism, Eupsychian management, etc. Gradually, my students move to this line of thinking. A good way is to get them to think of "school spirit" and what it really means. Is it an analogous way of speaking about a school and its effects on people, or is it a metaphysical reality, i.e., a being to which real loyalty is properly given with incredible results vis-à-vis student

and teacher productivity? Are teachers and students being moved by school spirit or being moved by nothing at all? If by the latter, then perhaps the skeptics in the school who denigrate the school leaders for their *esprit* are correct. The football team, the debate team, the science club, etc. . . are all "hype" and hardly worthy of participation if school spirit is really a "propaganda" tool of the school officials as they *dupe* the cooperators. This type of thinking begins to loosen the left side of their brains and the right side begins to take over with its holistic grasp of reality in a nonlogical way.

12. A quick reading of the popularizations in modern physics should relieve us of any embarrassing feelings regarding our seemingly ever proliferating lists of educational variables. Indeed, in the world of subatomic physics, it seems that particles are constantly being thought to be the "basics" only to be replaced again by new basics.

13. This is the ashram which is responsible for the periodical *Revision*, cited above.

Excerpts from

THE APPERCEPTIVE MASS

Excerpts from "The Confiteor"
What looks like an emerging new picture of the world to come
is just a change in the angle of vision we are given on the globe spinning in the invisible web of values that are eternal.

****

The big picture is, of course, not a big picture because there is no other picture. So the only picture is that fact that no-matter or anti-matter what, God wins. And what the heaven I am doing here is the "so what" puzzle

which hopefully solved would get me to the end of this
seemingly unendless poem.

* *

We are after all Christ . . . all of us
. . . and we are, after all, therefore, the anti-Christ which
is not a negative term as you can see. It is being positively
discovered about electrons negatively considered and there
is no need for any, but there is consolation in the scientific laboratory fact. And, if you don't believe me, did
you know physicists say there is a machine in the heart
of our galaxy causing everything to happen? Well, of course
there
is and a well-oiled processing of three parts it is and
that much must seem not queer mathematics but great. It's
about time.

* *

Excerpt from "The Sermon"
. . .
and let us say
we thank you
for the end of the tyranny of
objective science
and its now disenfranchised
removal of us persons from the
play of the universal game
and we glory in the
announcement of its demise
and now that the end of the world has appeared
witnessed as it was for each of us

judged
the new one will appear growing, as usual,
out of the ground in the new and
everlasting eden expressway
in the form of a subway tree
with all of us arching our back
to look up and see the arriving trains
of thought which go to build the
descending from the heavens
finally realized city of god

****

Excerpts from "Preface Ending in E"
I don't feel so bad
now that I know
time is warped too

****

Ah, granulated you and granulated me
losers all
reveling in this preconsecration in the paucity of
matter us which charged with the speed of light
and multiplied out yields us with this preface
ending in E for energy in this
multi-receipted poli-rejected hardly concepted
critically passed on
apperceptive
mass
the MC is about to arrive squared with the realities
of our day to day taken
lightly

****

Excerpt from "The Consecration"
Ah my host
my sacred flat sphere
you with your all-child radius
white hole of the universe
three in one truly singularity
through which, known, the other two
realities are known
witnessing in this sacred sign
of seven-in-one
the ever processing immutable
trinity models for all times
the truths of eternity
enhanced by models of science past, present, and future
the mystery of this freely resistible force

****

"Post Communion Prayer"
I still hurt inside from my childhood terrors
and my adult life is such that sometimes I don't
believe a thing so that the Heisenberg Principle
of indeterminacy is a consolation to those of us
who now-you-see-it-now-you-don't respond as
best we can sometimes even when we don't.
This best way to be is due to our weakness for
more than this could kill us which is no longer
necessary because if has all been done for
us and continues to be done for us even in
modes which confuse the mind and reality for in
truth there is no confusion possible in Christ
our lord. Amen.

* *

"Blessing"
let us not be cross at ourselves
for all the parts we have missed
for this is a function of the
angle of vision and angels too
go out into the uncaring world now
all you finally unweaned anawim
god weans ultimately
may you so receive
don't forget the bingo party
get home safely
I'm going to
San Salvador

Letter X

Dear Jim,

Here is another "extra" letter. The purpose of this one is to explain the hiatus between it and the last epistle. Thanks for the deadline extension . . . I think . . . and here's a hope that I can finish these letters by Easter . . . although it is only nine months to Christmas.

The delay in the writing was occasioned by a deeply personal event in my life. Thanks to the event, a slow process seems to have been instigated which consists of deprogramming and jettisoning some excess emotional baggage which has indeed functioned as *impedimenta*. Much "work" in the Gurdjiev sense of the word, remains to be done. The dark horse of Plato's charioteer has felt the whip of reason and now bucks and bolts much less than before and even shows signs of acquiescing to the will of the driver.

Now what all this has to do with these letters and their delay rests in the fact that among those things jettisoned . . . at least temporarily . . . was my Christianity . . . as hard as that seems for me to believe. The temporary jettisoning of Christianity was aided and abetted by my further investigation of some modern interpreters of quantum physics to the point that at one point in time I was apologizing to my Christian friends for my onslaught of Hinduism. I am afraid that all this might

200

sound a bit "flakey" or cavalier, but it's the best I can do to describe the situation.

At the time of the writing of this letter I am back again comfortable with Christianity, but I see it in a personalized way that I have never experienced and in a metaphysical way that is best described as a combination of East and West. I am, at this point in time, quite happy about all this although not totally devoid of uneasiness. Indeed, the easing of my original uneasiness has led me to the point where I can resume these letters. In addition to letting you know of my "reborn again" status, I think I should brief you on a few more things that have occurred relative to our last letters and to those to come.

Yesterday, I met David Bruce Duncan in front of the Wyeth "Night Sleeper" at the Metropolitan Museum of Art. Bruce McPherson from the University of Illinois and I were visiting the museum and David popped on by with a young teacher. Both of us wanted to share this incredible Wyeth with good friends. David indicated again his willingness to allow the use of his collage "Holy Family" for the book's cover. In light of the paintings "Wu Li" qualities and the opportunity it gives the viewer to correlate its information any number of ways, only one of which yields the figures of the "Holy Family" with Christ presented in the energy symbol, the painting seems even more relevant now to the book than before. Hope you agree. If you don't, if a reader is interested, he or she should feel free to stop by and take a "look see."

Bruce, by the way, has agreed to write a 'Foreword' for this series of letters so you can see that the trip to the museum was a real winner!

Also jettisoned in the deprogramming, reprogramming process was my chairmanship of the YMCA. Much as I love Uptown . . . and I have volunteered to return after Easter if I can be of help . . . I discovered that I was much too preoccupied with my personal side, these letters, and other publishing projects including the special edition of the *California Journal of Teacher Education* on religious education.

By the way, in that regard the article you wrote as the "overview" is a knockout and the best thing of yours I have read. It is concise, sharp, vigorous, scholarly, and challenging. Thank you very much. I am sure that if you publish it as a separate piece it will be a big hit. It certainly filled our bill . . . and more. Jim Stone at Berkeley was as delighted as I when he read your article and the others therein. Thanks again. I only hope these letters meet with half of such enthusiasm on your part.

For Promise, and vis-à-vis Egypt, I am soliciting funds to bring teachers, supervisors, and administrators from Catholic schools across the country to the Middle East. The American Association of Professors for Peace in the Middle East, of which I am associate treasurer, has been involved in such activities with public schools for many years. The thought of this new Promise project is to extend the same opportunity systematically to the Catholic schools. Jerry Starratt and Vin Dimunico, Jesuit contacts, have aided us in linking in the network of Jesuit schools along with twelve diocesan school systems (potentially) across the country. Should be fun. Want to come along if we get funded?

As far as Egypt itself goes, my last word from Zagazig was that the proposal was still being "processed" and that I could expect a visit, here, from them. To date, however, nothing much more has materialized. I sure wish it would.

Finally, I have managed to finish the poem which seeks to fuse Eastern and Western religion, physics, astronomy, and psychology . . . among other things. It is called the "Apperceptive Mass." Excerpts precede this letter. In the next letter, I'll write the promised "potpourri" letter on "unsolved issues" and then move on to an attempt at a letter of summary and/or conclusion. Thanks for your patience.

Holonomically yours,
David

Letter XI

March 29, 1982

Dear Jim,

Princess Di is pregnant. Jack Abbot, Norman Mailer's ex-offender protegé has been found guilty of murder. Since last I wrote a "regular" letter we've all been progressively recovering from the shooting of the Pope, President Reagan, President Sadat, and somebody has detected the existence of a gravity wave. It's been a busy time.

This letter is promised as a look at what I call some "unsolved problem areas." By that I mean I hope to discuss some areas of concern to religious education which are currently relevant and which I think might be viewed through the perspective of these letters, perhaps to some avail.

Authority

I think it safe to assume that teachers today, and especially teachers in religion, have a problem vis à vis authority. Teachers are faced with the attitude of their students, especially the young, who all too often show few signs of accepting the authority of the institution the teacher represents, or that of the teacher himself, or herself.

What all teachers, especially religious education teachers, are faced with is actually the problem of the moral development which must ensue if any individual learner is to cope in a highly structured society.

In these letters thus far, if there is a glaring ommission it is their failure to mention the whole notion of our students' moral development. I am aware of the contributions Kohlberg has made in this regard, and I certainly do not feel adequate to either summarize him or to go beyond him. Yet, our considerations thus far have been in large part derived from sources whose very "initial" problem is the problem of authority, morals, and social control. I am speaking of course about our social science deliberations in letters three and four. Their wellspring is the work of men like Weber, Parsons, Durkheim, etc. who found in religion the source of the morals, values, and value complexes which shape, mold, fine-tune, and basically sustain (i.e., keep from flying apart) our cultural institutions.

I would like to address this heritage and what it can bring to the authority dilemma of religious education. In doing so, I am going to roam freely through Chester Barnard's motifs in *The Functions of the Executive* without explicit citation. (I know how much you love citations. You even talk in footnotes sometimes.) I will point out that the following considerations are derived from Barnard's chapter 12, on "authority," and chapter 17, on "leadership," or "executive" responsibility. I think constant citation would impede the flow of the "argument."[1]

AUTHORITY AND MORAL DEVELOPMENT

Young people today are uncannily aware, it seems to me, of who really is in control in an instructional setting, wherever this setting might be. They are! To be more specific, and Barnard can help us here, they are aware as he is that authority never resides in those called "authorities." Thus, the teacher whom common sense identifies as the authority, is, according to Barnard, not the authority at all. For authority has very much to say to the "acceptance" of a communication. As a matter of fact the willingness to process and act according to received communications is a fair way of encapsulating what Barnard refers to as "subjective authority." At the same time, this acceptance, this subjective authority, is matched by objective authority which is the character of the communication which establishes the acceptance. At no time does authority reside in those called the teacher, i.e., in the "authority," so-called.

I have already recommended a prehensive curriculum for religious education. If it is anything, it is a richly *experiential* curriculum and very prominent in the curriculum is the whole notion of career education. And you will remember that the purpose of career education was ultimately the enhancement of the probability that the learner will achieve openness, and transcendence. This comes about through experiencing the world of organized work which is itself a vast ocean of moral codes of the workplace.

The notion of the world of work as a vast complex of moral codes may seem at first a bit strange. But, in truth and in Barnard's theory, it is. He is quick to point out that until an individual achieves an appreciation of an organization as a function of intricate, complex, multivariate moral codes painstakingly adhered to, that individual will not see organization for what it is and therefore will not be fit for top executive positions. In other words, Barnard's whole treatise, culminating as we pointed out in the experience of transcendence for the contributor, presents organized working life as a rich mesh of moral codes. He goes so far as to demonstrate that until one sees, for example, the cobbler at his bench or the marketing director at her desk as functions of powerful moral codes, one will not grasp the essence of organization and therefore be ill-equipped to function as a manager or leader therein.

On the practical side of things, in exposing religious education students to the workplace, while its ultimate rationale is to lead them to working and transcending, we should be mindful that transcendence is achieved through "buying in" to (i.e., accepting the authority of) moral codes of the workplace which range from pride of craft to honesty, integrity, and courage, etc. My friends in management are eager to point out that organizations can be looked at very heuristically as decision-making structures, but, alas, what many of them fail to see is that the *guts* of the matter is the *moral decision-making* process which, when rightly aimed, enhances transcendence although it can also be the source of the ulcers.

The nice part about all this is that it is not too hard to get most young people to accept the teaching authority of experience in the workplace. Even the ex-offenders I have dealt with have readily come to appreciate the plusses of the workplace in getting their act together and the death-dealing blows they do to themselves in this regard when their disco, sex, and drug habits interfere with their legitimate participation therein. They even seem to be able to process, somewhat, the fact that the workplace as we know it today is not a paradigm of virtuous behavior. But, at least they see first-hand what is going on and *feel* the difference between right and wrong.

Moral development is acquired, then, in experience in the workplace through an authority which, perhaps initially because of its material reward, in part is accepted by the learner. To experience the workplace is to experience right and wrong and to realize ultimately, perhaps after many years, that one's basic need for transcendence can be viably met there. Included in the moral learnings of the workplace are the sexual moral learnings.

SEX

First off, proving I have at least a grasp of the obvious, there *has been* a sexual revolution. Chalk it up to drugs, Vietnam, whatever, the sexual mores which surround us have undergone a radical change. And, the revolution took place across all classes . . . or just about.

I recently was on the 79th Street crosstown bus to the Metropolitan Museum of Art (where else?), and two young chaps come in, sat down, and continued their matter-of-fact, unanimated, almost clinical discussion of the difference between oral sex between persons of the same sex and persons of opposite sexes. The topic did not surprise me. What remains forever with me is the matter-of-fact attitude these middle-schoolers (private school, well-heeled, and all that) exhibited.

At the other end of the class scale, the young people I deal with on the upper Westside here exhibit the same attitude, more or less, and live in an environment of sex which knows few if any taboos. In both cases it is not that there are no moral codes in evidence regarding sexual behavior. Indeed, the code is one of intense individual decision not only as to what one does sexually but as to the immorality of institutions trying to stifle individual creativity in this regard.

The point I am making here is not whether this is a healthy development or not; the point is it's a real phenomenon, of recent vintage, and one cannot seriously deal with the adolescent of my experience without, in most cases, coming squarely in touch with what is a complex sexual ethic of individualism, voluntary sharing, and societal justice in things sexual. It comes with a knowledge-base most adequate to support it.

On the adult side, Roxie Hart's girlfriend, Velma Kelly, in the show *Chicago,* observes, "Everybody you watch, has his brains in his crotch." The observation certainly does seem true and accurate. The obsession we in America have with sex is remarkable. And I guess that is another reason I feel it appropriate to talk about it in these letters. Another reason for looking at sex and the religious education teacher is the close connection between the two "phenomena." I notice that in your overview of the religion/education interface which you wrote for the *California Journal of Teacher Education,* you start with an analogy between the deeply personal ramifications of religion and the deeply personal ramifications of sex. While I do not agree with your conclusion (which disagreement does not effect the wonderful solid sweep of your argument's flow in the rest of the article), I can point out that even in the "literature" the connection between sex and religion is unmistakable.

Still another reason for discussion of sex in these letters stems from some earlier thoughts, specifically the thoughts on career education in a prehensive, moral development curriculum for religious instruction. To enmesh students in the world of work is to enmesh them in a sexually infused environment. The fascination with sex naturally spills over into the workplace. The large organizations that I have worked for certainly evidenced no exceptionality in this regard. The fact that more than one job was assigned, more than one raise achieved, and more than one firing effected by suburban bedroom action on a cold winter night eludes none. Is this anything to introduce a child to?

I am writing about sex, not because I am any expert on the subject. Indeed, I was "spirited" through puberty by a German Roman Catholic ethos before I found out what it was. As a friend of long-standing you are no stranger to my sexual interludes and my heretofore inability to bring them to any satisfactory, long-lasting resolve. So I merit writing on this topic not because of any personal achievement in this regard, but because I have observed its operation in the real world of work.

These, then, are my reasons for introducing the topic of sex. They all come down to the fact that the workplace is sexual, and a religious education program rich in exposure to careers will eventually find itself faced with the topic. And it is a thorny topic. No two organized religions seem to agree on the topic. Tenets range from those that propose celibacy as the ideal to those that preach salvation through "excess." So the last thing I am going to do is take a position in this regard—no pun intended. I am, however, going to share my observations of sex in the workplace, hopefully focus some relevant concepts germane to these letters on the phenomenon, and alert religion education teachers to the sexual education resource the workplace has always been to achieve the introjection of whatever code of ethics in this regard.

I hope my observations and suggestions, will be universal enough to apply across the board. I am told Alice Roosevelt Longworth articulated the following empirical generalization of sexual behavior: "Fill what is empty and empty what is filled." Whatever you happen to think is empty and in need of filling, whatever you think is full and warrants emptying . . . or whatever you think shouldn't be emptied and whatever you think shouldn't be filled, etc. . . . that's not the issue. What is the issue is how the workplace can be viewed in all its sexual ramification in a way that your own particular sexual curriculum can be developed and delivered.

While I hope you can see the merits in this universal approach (if I can pull it off) I think you can also see the merits as far as the teachers own sexual needs are concerned. As per our discussion above, the real teacher is now in a very real way *experience* and the individual teacher's personal sexual proclivities and activities are not at issue . . . theoretically, anyway.

The teacher, vis à vis the student, is not an authority in sexual or any other matter per se. I am not saying that institutional role expectations on the sexual activity of religious education teachers are not real and potent. Certainly many sects and cults "model" their own ideal sexual behavior through their teachers and insist on it being so. But my own experience with this type of "modeling" leads me to suspect it's basic effectiveness, nice as it is for some to think about. Indeed, from within my own religious "training" in this regard, I can't recall too many of us who thought that our mentors were authorities in sex. It was quite the opposite. For us, the authority was in the street, the butcher shop, the bakery, the auto garage. That's where the action is, that's where the teaching goes on. That's where sexual moral codes are learned and therefore that's where religious education teachers should be with their students, directly or indirectly.

So now that we've taken the pressure off the teacher somewhat, let's look at the influence of sex in the workplace. What might be helpful for religious education teachers to know so that as they venture forward thereonto they are not going in naively and willynilly.

A famous poet is said to have observed that as he came into his maturity all he really wanted out of life was a job, poetry, and sex life. Then, he met the enemy; a female sadistic bureaucrat. That's all it took to let him realize that his wants were not going to be met all that easily in the workplace.

Our poet's observation seems accurate; its sexual overtones are clear and it has introduced elements of sadism and bureaucracy. I think I have railed against bureaucracy enough in past letters, but the fact that many large organizations have become the nest of both male and female sadists seems worthy of note.

And being the good "little" Freudian that I am, the sadism invariably springs from a sexual thwart, past, present, real, imagined, etc.

Now, at this point in time religious education teachers might be asking, again, "Is this any place to take a child?" Well, my answer is still "yes," but I'll have to bring back Chester Barnard to the rescue. Specifically, let's take a look at his concept of "informal organization," perhaps his most important contribution. If we understand this then we can see that the typical career education experience, short of continuous work experience, is in no danger of revealing the sexual and sadistic side of organized life. For what experiences, like field trips, yield is a very salubrious and heuristic view of formal organization. And is there anything more sexless? Even the Playboy organizational chart looks dry as dust, and the local gas station, while perhaps a bit grubby, at most has a Vargas calendar on display, and its own business forms and reports match those of Playboy's in their impersonal tone.

Formally, then, organizations are nonsexual to the point of sterility. And this is usually the first exposure children get, and the variety of formal organizations is such that many such sexless exposures are very useful. But, as Barnard points out, no organization runs according to its charts. There is a "hidden government," and this complex of human interactions he calls the informal organization. You can't see that written up anywhere. You can only feel it through experience. Like Freud's unconscious vis à vis the individual, this informal organization is a powerful shaper of organizational behavior, although most of the time you never even hear talk about it. It is there. And religious education teachers might well realize that it is, with or without their input, a force in the workplace which is in many instances quite sexual.

No one is surprised to learn of the sexual "underside" of the local auto garage. There is no reason to be surprised that there is a sexual underside to a large bureaucracy. What may surprise us is the power of this sexual underside. In some cases the informal runs the formal.

What, then, is a religious education teacher to do? There he or she is, faced on the one hand with sexually hip kids and on the other with a sexually infused workplace. All this while one's institutional expectations and one's own sexual life are crying for attention.

Prayer helps some. Still others discover that Barnard's concept of *informal organization* applies to their own institution as well in all probability. That is just to say that *formal* institutional expectations regarding, for example, extramarital sex, are quite clear and unmistakeable, but *informally* the situation is much more fluid. Curiously, I think the kids pick this up before the teachers. *That* they will buy. Taking this under consideration, a religious education teacher soon learns that things, even at "home," are not quite what they appear.

But, you say, doesn't this call for a hypocritical posture on the part of the teacher . . . or worse, on the part of the institution. Well, yes and no. Is that a subatomic particle? Well, yes and no. Sometimes it looks like a particle, sometimes it looks like a wave, and sometimes it doesn't show up. Is solving sexual dilemmas and creative code making regarding sex hypocritical when one utilizes the informal approach? Well, yes and no. If extramarital sex is not okay, then say so. But, on the other hand, if extramarital sex is okay sometimes, then don't say so formally. Why not? Well, sometimes it's best to leave the formal where it is. You will admit this whole issue is like tracking electrons in a lab. There is certain indeterminacy here and quite possibly, by *principle*. There is out there no one moral "formula" always available. But there is always a complementarity between the formal and the informal tenets.

Well, now that I may have lost all the absolute moralists out there let me point out that all I want to do is bring some motifs to bear on what is a big decision-making problem for teachers of religions charged with inculcating sexual mores, especially mores of the traditional nature. And I can observe that religious education teahers seem to operate in this way.

The story of Christ and the woman taken in adultery comes to mind. The locals wanted to stone her in what was a clear-cut, formal instance of the breaking of the formal law. At stake, then, is a question of law. At this point, for the only time I know of, Christ writes . . . and he writes in the sand. After he writes, he delivers the famous, "Let him who is without sin cast the first stone." They draw back, the woman gets up, and Christ says something to the effect that she is free to go and she should commit this sin no more.

Note the attitude Christ takes, not only toward sex but toward the law. Toward the sex, he seems matter-of-fact; toward the law he is saying, as I am interpreting it, that the law is like writing, writing not in stone, but in sand. Is it possible he wanted us to view the law in a somewhat "looser," granular (holonomic?) indeterminate fashion as opposed to the hard-fast, formal institution comedown on the individual sinner? Note, too, how this great teacher used his knowledge of his local institutions' informal sexual shenanigans in his ministry and teaching. He knew the omnipresence of sexual activity in the tacit, informal network.

Religious career education, then, has great potential for teaching sexual mores. In all probability the "testier" issues will not surface per se until some sort of work experience becomes a part of this program. It is then that the overheard phone conversation to the abortionist, the homosexual pass, and the spurned and vengeful boss will begin to play their part in a young person's eyes. At least such an experience will save our children from the naive entry of a hapless poet into the workplace. At best, however, it will provide the "fodder" of moral development—across the board, yes—but also, and perhaps even especially, sexually.

One final point comes to mind. I seem to present the influence of sex in the workplace as negative. This certainly has been my experience in the main. It need not always be so and is not. Perfectly classic marriages and viable relationships come from the workplace, too, and the fact that they do fills many a junior executive position from year to year, with both males and females. In general, though, the overall impact informal organizations seem to be having, from the auto industry to our schools seems to be negative. One wonders, then, if a serendipitous effect may be had by introducing the career prehensive curriculum in education in this regard. Might not the presence of fresh, young, learning minds, ever quick to discriminate between pompous hypocrisy and legitimate informal action help our corporations and bureaucracies dust off their moral roots to the benefit of upping productivity? How's that for dreaming? Still, watch what the presence of youngsters does in a workplace. Intriguing, no?

THE MORAL MAJORITY

While there are those who would denigrate the importance of sexual mores, there are also those who rally to traditional sexual values from what they see as ravages by the new sexual ambience. Among these latter one can place the Moral Majority. In a very real sense they can be viewed as being in a "tractive"[2] leadership posture in today's culture . . . tractive because they are dusting off, polishing, and emphasizing traditional values that they fear are in danger . . . at least that is what I think they think they are doing. I'd like to discuss the Moral Majority in light of the motifs we've touched on in these letters.

I wonder, for example, what the Moral Majority's response would be to the emphasis placed herein on transcendence. Would they agree that the object of religious education is the altered, transcendental state of consciousness? I think they would. For the fervor and power of their presentations, and the large group one-mindedness they engender in their gatherings reveal that they, too, know the power of the need to transcend. And this fact brings us to observe that transcendence as an objective of religious experience or as *the* religious experience is prominently on display in contemporary American circles. Friends of mine who cannot understand the appeal of the Moral Majority fail to see the powerful linking of individuals to something readily available that is bigger than themselves, something with which they can identify and thereby lose themselves to find themselves, born again fresh and new.

I wonder, too, if what they are saying is really what they mean? The "abuses" they seek to eliminate from American society, e.g., sexual promiscuity, homosexuality, etc., are hardly new phenomena. Isn't what they are really reacting to the fact that what has always been *informally* (and significantly) present is now present formally, i.e., in the media, liberation movements, etc.

In this light, then, the Moral Majority seems to be a voice raised, although not in so many words, for a code governing the relationship between the formal and the informal. This code seems to spring from an innate sense that moral matters like physics particles are somewhat indeterminate. Viewed in this light, this code "regulates" what people should accept formally and what people should accept informally. I don't know if you find these thoughts helpful. But from the perspective of a religious education teacher in a very pluralistic society, I think the transcendental qualities of the Moral Majority experiences and an appreciation of the informal organization in moral judgment and behavior helps to get a clearer fix on what is happening. Perhaps approaching the Moral Majority on the *shared basis* of transcendence and the possible *real point of contention,* i.e., the code governing formal/informal balance, would improve the dialog between them and those among us who do not agree with them.

The Organization of Religious Education

Well, I hope this look at the Moral Majority phenomenon and the religious education in terms of social science was at least interesting and perhaps practical in its implications for improved dialog. Now we come to the next issue. It is the organization of the religious education enterprise. I think I would like to write a book about this because the considerations we have shared seem to me to speak most importantly to management and organizational principles appropriate to religious instruction. Theoretically speaking, it seems to me that Barnard and Teilhard de Chardin should be linked along with Maslow, to form a management theory appropriate to a transcendence-oriented operation. All the wherewithal is there and it remains but to articulate the synthesis.

Practically, the work of Rensis Likert and his research underscoring the increased long-term productivity of Management Systems 3 and 4 would be most appropriate.[3] These systems can be characterized by their meeting of workers' (i.e., teachers') needs, with "system four" seeming to be the way to go to enhance the probability of the workers' self-fulfillment all the way to transcendence. Certainly systems 1 and 2, smacking as they so much do of ratio-technical principles and fixated as they are at the lower needs levels, are to be avoided.

Organizations consequently would in the main be very flat, with the teacher freed to, in effect, run the enterprise. Evaluation would be by more humanistic modes like artifacts and portfolio analysis. Certainly a prehensive religious teacher would have an impressive collection of things, tapes, pictures, student artistic achievements, etc. to amply demonstrate productivity. Finally, the very locale of instruction is seen as disparate and enmeshed in the scientific, artistic, and general career worlds in which we live and learn about transcendence and its personal, moral prerequisites. Such organization and management Bruce McPherson and I tentatively call *transmanagement,* and we have already worked out an outline for a book about it in the public sector.

CHURCH-STATE

Mentioning the public sector leads me to the final issue of this potpourri chapter. It is the issue of the church/state or religion/public school interface. Once again I can simply refer the reader to your excellent lead article in the spring 1982 edition of the *California Journal of Teacher Education.* But over and above all that, I would like to remark that, in terms of this series of letters to you the failure of public education to meet the need for transcendence on the part of teachers and students alike is at the heart of its lowered productivity.

I know of your own popularity as a young teacher, and I am sure you haven't forgotten the transcendence of a "good day"—that incredibly wonderful feeling when you and the class joined as one and explored some reality in a perfect orchestration of discovery and insight. We all need this, but teachers especially need this. It is *the* reward in teaching; it is that aspect of teaching that is ineffable, telling about which is nigh on to impossible, and that part about teaching that non-teachers are most unfamiliar with. Why do they forget those moments they had as students? Why do they not see this as the reward reality gives to the most important people in any society . . . the teachers?

So bad is the situation in our schools, sustained by unbelievable insensitive bureaucrats, that, far from transcendence, the greatest need teachers have today is self-esteem. So low is their own self-esteem as teachers that they are loathe to have their own children enter their chosen profession; so low is their self-esteem that they project it on their colleagues and prefer to socialize with anyone else *but* teachers. They look down at themselves, they look down on one another, and, worst of all, society looks down on them.

In simple terms: no transcendence, no ultimate satisfaction, no continuing and increasing effectiveness.

The problem with the public schools in very real terms is a religious one. They are not designed to meet this ultimate need of teachers and, in turn, the students are not provided with the wherewithal to meet their own needs for transcendence. That's a good way to induce, at best, boredom, at worst, social alienation. In this latter regard, the possibility that the schools have become a social menace rather than a generator of social stability and positive growth is very real.

It's too easy to blame the bureaucrats as I have and will probably continue to do. It's probably more *ad rem* to blame you and me for our participation in what looks to me like an abandoning of teachers by those who prepare them, and by their administrators. Where is their champion? Where is their cultural voice? Why have we permitted this demeaning of our teachers to occur? Is it them we hate, or is it a necessary consequence that a culture in which emergent values of instant gratification are rapidly developing must necessarily if unconsciously *hate* its young and therefore dismiss as irrelevant their teachers?

After all, if *carpe diem* is the name of the game, how do children fit in except as current or future competitors? You can't appreciate children if you are not long-range in your value outlook. Most religions are long-range. We need religious values for our children. We need religious values, at least as defined in this book, in our schools. We must look at this religion-public school interface again. The wall between church and state which removes religion from the schools is a law that makes for a lousy curriculum. We are living with the results.

Time to close. The Oscars have been awarded. The Columbia has landed, and I'm up for writing a last letter to you. I hope this potpourri chapter hasn't been too random. It functions as kind of a sample of how the thoughts in the previous letters can be brought to bear on some current goings on. Hope you and religious education teachers find it helpful.

YOURS AND NOT YOURS (IN A COMPLEMENTARITY SENSE)
DAVID

Notes to Letter XI

1. Chester I. Barnard, *The Functions of the Executive* (Cambridge: Harvard University Press, 1938), pp. 114–123.

2. Ben M. Harris, *Supervisory Behavior in Education* (Englewood Cliffs, N.J.: Prentice-Hall, Inc., 1963), p. 21.

3. Rensis Likert, *The Human Organization: Its Management and Value* (New York: McGraw-Hill, 1967).

Letter XII

Where does the east meet the west?
At sunset there is a choice of two smiles; discreet or serious.
In this best of all possible worlds, that is enough.

John Ashbery, "The Serious Doll"

Dear Jim,

I am writing this last letter to you during Holy Week, 1982. I'll indicate which day of Holy Week it is as the letter proceeds.

I suddenly realized that it would be a mistake for me to try to sum up what I have tried to say in these letters. I am reminded of a story, apocryphal perhaps, of Thomas Aquinas and his refusal to finish the *Summa* when requested to do so by his superiors. It seems he had a transcendental experience which rendered it nigh on to impossible for him to finish up his *comprehensive* approach to religion. Indeed, in referring to the *Summa* he referred to it, after his experience, as "straw." I will save you the twentieth century equivalent of thirteenth century "straw." But in this little vignette I see the germs of the value of a *prehensive* approach to religious education as opposed to a comprehensive approach.

PASSOVER

The unison of the knights
revering the holy blood
unfolds the ultimate
emulsion of
our fundamental unity
in one blood
and in the Christian ritual of
particle bread and wave blood
the double appearances of the same thing
which is it which it is
unites us in the sum of all appearances

this unison of special nights
makes this night special
as every other knight's night
is special and their ladies, too
beyond the illusion
is the real
wherein
the seeing is the being
and the being of

the elevated plane
reveals itself
as not elevated
since nought exists
to be elevated over

Indeed, no comprehensive approach is possible, for by that very approach you create a new prehension not subsumed under your "original comprehension." Hence, the impossibility of a *Summa* and hence the no-longer need of a new summa; rather, the need to *prehensively* act and build to the critical mass in each learner to effect the point of mystical titration . . . basing everything, of course, on the apperceptive mass of the teacher and learner.

And so I almost fell into a trap and thought this letter would be one of summation . . . as it were, a comprehension of everything that has gone before.

But what of the almost universal thrust in formal education for such a comprehension? Well, it is a useful exercise in a scientific mode. It reveals much that was not known before. But by its very seeking for closure, it makes most difficult the handling of motifs like transcendence. For ultimately, as the Thomas Aquinas vignette indicated, one even transcends the most comprehensive of works. If one does not, then one does not transcend.

By the way, the poem immediately above ("Passover") results from some ruminations on Passover and Holy Thursday occasioned by a trip to the Metropolitan Opera House to see Parsifal for the first time. Needless to say, "it" happened again, although it was again very different, and I am still pondering the "quantum jump" I experienced at the Holy Thursday scene in the second act.

Rather than sum up for you what I think has happened in these letters, I think that I will simply list what I think some of the most important thoughts I had were. My only criterion for the following selected "list" is my own sense of the thoughts' meaningfulness, practicality, etc. I'm sure even my own judgment in this regard is not all that hard-and-fast. Here's the list . . . with minimal annotation.

LIST OF MOST IMPORTANT THOUGHTS

1. Meet the needs of the teacher. Without this prehensive element, nothing much else can happen. Basically, of course, we are talking about the teacher's need to transcend.
2. Transcendence is the objective of religious education. Whether or not this thought will be seen as a helpful one for others, I do not know. For my own part, it enables me to look on learners in all kinds of settings knowing that just one touch of transcendence will change the whole picture for them and for me. Once in conversation you referred to this motif in the letters as a "corrective." Perhaps rather than corrective it is tractive, and ultimately will turn out to be another, needed perhaps, dusting off of some pretty old truths.
3. Achieving transcendence is facilitated by the social sciences, the arts, and the so-called "harder" sciences. Indeed, the thread of the letters which seems to be central is the leaps between and among science and the arts on the basis of their shared transcendental and transcendence-enhancing motifs.
4. The prehensive way of thinking about the religious education curriculum ultimately creates the prehensive learner. Indeed, to learn to is continuously prehend.
5. The methodology of these letters, naturalistic inquiry, is appropriate to the task of these letters because of its deeply personal mode. It is also a methodology appropriate to a generation of humans of ever increasing average age. For it respects the age and the experience of the individual inquirer and, in effect, says to the inquirer that he or she, because of innate prehensive qualities, is a more valuable information storage and retrieval system

than any computer and its bank. As we grow older together, the more we can share more and more experience. The knowledge explosion is not in the amassing of facts or the creation of technological "know how" at a rapid rate; rather *we* are the knowledge explosion . . . we ourselves. It is, after all, wonderful to grow old, always moving from being prehensile to prehensive.

6. Moral education, including sexual moral development, occurs in the workplace to a most significant degree. To view the workplace as a holographic meshed matrix of moral codes helps to see its potential and its reality in the moral formation, not only of youth, but of adults also. I think it was John Gardner who pointed out that if our intellectuals look down on our plumbers and our plumbers look down on our intellectuals, then . . . and perhaps this is what we are experiencing now . . . both our plumbing and our theories will leak. Christ the placenta . . . yes; but Christ the carpenter, too.

I think I'll stop at six. And I'll close this last letter to you with the thoughts that seem to be filling my head and the feelings that are surfacing.

CLOSING THOUGHTS AND FEELINGS

It's Holy Saturday, and I remember now how I got here, formally anyway. It all started with Sister Mary Bernadette in the first grade at Blessed Sacrament School in Cleveland. She asked the class, "What are the three most important parts of the Mass?" I felt my hand shoot up and heard myself saying "Offertory, Consecration, and Communion." I can still see where I was sitting. In back of me was the place in the class where we erected a store. We stocked the store with foods which we "created" in art sessions. Thus, for example, we would fashion apples and oranges out of clay, paint them, most decoratively as I recall, and then display them for purchase in the bins of the simulated grocery shop. I even remember that I never did get to run the store but, somehow, that was okay by me, and I even think I understood that my not running the store was insignificant. I still was having a good time. What a wonderful teacher!

How I loved her and how she loved us. But even she knew, along with Bruno Bettleheim that love is not enough, witness the fact that I also recall her grabbing me by the hand, putting a piece of chalk in my hand, lifting me by the hand off my feet, up to the top of the blackboard and swinging my whole body in the figure of a 6, realizing that so recalcitrant a nature at times required a very physical approach to learning. Have you ever swung through the air in the shape of a six while chalking a huge six on a blackboard? I'm sure she did it, realizing that unless I mastered *six,* I would blow her lesson on the *seven* sacraments. Whatever, it's all there in my own first-grade education.

The arts, the workplace, etc. in the care of a teacher whose needs were met so she could meet mine. Pretty lucky, wouldn't you say?

Curiously, though, I continue ofttimes to cower and ofttimes I don't let my hand shoot up. A case in point was my psych course with Bruno Bettelheim. I remember him asking, "Did Freud invent psychoanalysis?" and myself saying, to myself, "No, Freud did not invent psychoanalysis. Plato knew all about it as is evidenced by the dark and light horses of the charioteer." I was so cowed by the very presence of the man, even though I was in the last row of students in the auditorium, that I did not answer his question, except to myself. Bruno's was the one class I never said a word out loud in, in my entire student career. Needless to say, that *was* the answer Bruno wanted.

And as I have written these letters I alternated, in good complementarity fashion, between enthusiastically shooting my hand up and cowering, wishing the back row was even farther away. Poised as I have been these last two years or more between relishing this writing and, in effect, coweringly dreading this writing, I can only wonder what it will be like to have the letters finished. Well, I guess I am about to find out.

Holy Saturday
David

It's noon. Easter is here. Mike Lewis, Fr. Paul's nephew is in from Princeton and we are heading over to the Frick Museum. I saw one of the Berrigans on Broadway yesterday in a nuclear march. I think he got arrested. I love the "nuclear theology" of some of the bishops who are helping to stabilize this antinuclear war "processing." I think if I were to start these letters all over again, that's where I would jump into the "conversation" with you. I wonder why?

Thanks to John Ashbery, I can leave you in good, albeit somewhat muted, vaudeville style, with "a choice of two smiles" . . . I realize that this is a somewhat indeterminate way of signing off but, I am sure you can see that it is complementarity in action. I would love it if these letters have brought a smile to your lips and to our readers lips. And, it would be too much to ask that it be, at least, a "serious" smile; but if it isn't, I hope it can at least be a "discreet" smile. What better way to respond to a Walter Mitty of religious or any other kind (is there any other kind) of education?

Well, "in this best of all possible worlds, that is enough."

Love you more than ever,
David

P.S.

The madonna brown sweeps through the celestials
pregnant she comes again with the savior of mankind
the battle has been won once and for all
but the residuals who hide from the light are
given this second coming, this second helping
how like god to take his creatures' way
the children play and the folds of her gown
brown are a delight for them . . . is that
why they seem so cherubic
and the last eternal supper goes on
and we all cannot help but be saved
being necessarily there
and unworthy though we be in this unworthiness
is the face of the Christ on the way of the cross
through which we all gain eternal life
and though none will read this as I write it
it matters little as little does
for someone once said that little things
mean a lot but so do big things for
everything folden golden means
even the extremes to which we are all brought
bought . . . perhaps
but in the center is that eliotian elysian stillness in need of
no editor

D.

Index of Names

229

Index of Subjects